DISPLACED BY DEVELOPMENT: THE POLITICAL ECONOMY OF JHARKHAND

VIVEK KUMAR HIND

Dedicated to marginalized tribal communities in Jharkhand .

Contents

Foreword

The history of development in postcolonial India is inextricably intertwined with the fate of its most marginalized communities—those whose lands, cultures, and identities have been the collateral damage of the state's relentless pursuit of modernity and economic growth. *Displaced by Development: The Political Economy of Jharkhand* is a timely and essential contribution to our understanding of these paradoxes. In this powerful work, Vivek Kumar Hind brings critical attention to the lived realities of development-induced displacement, with a focus on one of India's most resource-rich yet persistently impoverished regions—Jharkhand.

This book does more than document the displacement of Adivasi and other vulnerable communities; it interrogates the very foundations of how we conceptualize development. Hind asks the uncomfortable but necessary questions: What is the cost of progress? Who decides its trajectory? And who are the invisible victims left behind in its wake? Drawing from a rich blend of theoretical frameworks—including modernization theory, the capability approach, and political economy—this work challenges dominant narratives that equate infrastructure and industrialization with national success.

What sets this volume apart is its deep grounding in both rigorous scholarship and empathetic field engagement. The author's connection to the land and people of Jharkhand, combined with years of academic inquiry, makes this a work of both intellectual depth and ethical urgency. Hind brings to life the voices and struggles of displaced communities, mapping the contours of loss, resilience, and resistance with clarity and compassion.

Jharkhand is not merely a regional case study here—it is a crucible in which the broader contradictions of India's development strategy are laid bare. Through detailed analysis of mining, dam construction, land acquisition policies, and community mobilization, the book highlights how displacement is not a peripheral issue but a central feature of contemporary capitalism and statecraft. At the same time, it illuminates paths toward more inclusive and sustainable alternatives rooted in justice, participation, and ecological sensitivity.

This book will be of immense value to scholars of development studies, political economy, public policy, and South Asian studies, as well as to practitioners, policymakers, and activists committed to social justice. It is both an indictment of the dispossessive logic of extractive development and a call to reimagine progress in ways that center the rights and aspirations of those most often excluded from its benefits.

Displaced by Development is not just a book—it is an intervention, an act of solidarity, and an invitation to rethink the future of development in India and beyond.

Dr. Jagdish Prasad
Associate Professor & Head,
　University Department of Political Science,
　Tilka Manjhi Bhagalpur University, Bhagalpur
June 2025

Preface

The journey of this book Displaced by Development: The Political Economy of Jharkhandbegan with a simple but urgent question: What does development mean for those who are asked to sacrifice the most for its promise? In India, the pursuit of economic growth, industrialization, and infrastructural expansion has long been celebrated as a path to national progress. Yet, beneath the rhetoric of modernization and prosperity lies a more troubling reality—one marked by the large-scale displacement of millions, especially among Adivasis, Dalits, and small farmers. Their stories of loss, resilience, and resistance are often overshadowed by narratives of national achievement.

This book, Displaced by Development: The Political Economy of Jharkhand, seeks to bring these stories to the forefront. It is a critical exploration of the politics of displacement in India, with a particular focus on Jharkhand—a region that starkly illustrates the contradictions of resource-rich lands inhabited by resource-poor people. The manuscript interrogates the structures of power and policy that enable displacement, the theoretical frameworks that have shaped our understanding of development, and the lived experiences of communities who have borne the brunt of progress.

The work is rooted in the conviction that displacement is not merely a logistical or economic issue, but a deeply political and ethical one. It is about who decides what constitutes development, whose voices are heard, and whose interests are prioritized. The book draws on historical analysis, political economy, and rights-based perspectives to unravel how state policies, corporate interests, and global capital intersect to dispossess the most vulnerable. At the same time, it highlights the agency of displaced communities—how they resist, negotiate, and reimagine their futures in the face of adversity.

Jharkhand serves as both a case study and a symbol. With its vast mineral wealth and history of extractive development, the state exemplifies the paradoxes and perils of India's growth trajectory. It is here that the struggles for land, identity, and justice are most acute, and where the possibilities for alternative, more inclusive models of development are being articulated and tested.

This book does not offer easy answers. Instead, it raises fundamental questions about the meaning and purpose of development in a deeply unequal society. Who benefits from development, and who pays the cost? How can the rights, dignity, and agency of displaced communities be protected and promoted? What alternatives exist to the dominant paradigm of extractive, exclusionary growth?

The chapters that follow are the result of extensive research, fieldwork, and engagement with scholars, activists, and community members. They reflect a commitment to scholarship that is both rigorous and empathetic, critical and constructive. The hope is that this work will contribute to ongoing debates about development, justice, and democracy in India, and inspire readers to imagine a future in which progress does not come at the expense of the most vulnerable.

I am deeply grateful to all those who shared their stories, insights, and struggles with me. Their courage and resilience are the true inspiration behind this book. I also acknowledge the support of colleagues, mentors, and friends who encouraged and challenged me throughout this journey.

As India continues to chart its path toward modernization, it is imperative that we pause to ask: Progress for whom, and at what cost? This book is an invitation to reflect, question, and act—so that development may become a source of empowerment, not dispossession, for all.

Vivek Kumar Hind

Acknowledgements

Writing this book has been a journey shaped by many people, places, and experiences. As someone born in Madhupur, in the district of Deoghar, Jharkhand, and having spent much of my life in the tribal heartlands of Jharkhand and Chhattisgarh, the issues of displacement, development, and the struggles of indigenous communities have always been close to my heart. My academic path and personal experiences have both contributed to the making of this work.

First and foremost, I express my deepest gratitude to the tribal communities of Jharkhand and Chhattisgarh. Their resilience, wisdom, and struggles in the face of adversity have been my greatest teachers. Their stories—of loss, hope, and resistance—form the soul of this book. I am indebted to those who welcomed me into their villages, shared their lives, and trusted me with their narratives.

I am grateful to my colleagues and students at Tilka Manjhi Bhagalpur University, where I currently serve as Assistant Professor. Their engagement and encouragement have been invaluable. My previous tenures at Guru Ghasidas Central University, Bilaspur, and Government College Sanawal, Balrampur, under the Department of Higher Education, provided me with rich academic environments and opportunities to interact with diverse scholars and students. These institutions have played a significant role in shaping my academic vision and commitment to social justice.

I owe special thanks to my teachers and mentors at Banaras Hindu University (BHU), Varanasi, where I completed my higher education. The rigorous training and intellectual stimulation I received at BHU laid the foundation for my research and critical thinking. The values and perspectives I gained there continue to guide me in my academic pursuits.

I am also grateful to the many scholars, activists, and friends who have inspired and supported me over the years. Their insights, debates, and solidarity have enriched this work in countless ways. I would particularly like to acknowledge those who have dedicated their lives to the cause of tribal rights, social justice, and equitable development in India.

My family has been my unwavering support through the long process of research and writing. Their patience, understanding, and encouragement have made this book possible. I thank them for believing in my work and for sharing in my commitment to the issues that matter most to me.

Finally, I thank the readers who will engage with this book. It is my hope that this work will contribute to a deeper understanding of the politics of displacement in India and inspire further dialogue, research, and action for justice and inclusion.

Vivek Kumar Hind

Prologue

In the dense sal forests and mineral-laden soils of Jharkhand, the sound of progress often comes not as celebration, but as rupture. It echoes through the controlled blasts of dynamite in coalfields, the churning of earth for dam foundations, and the hum of machines that pave the roads to mines and factories. For the Adivasis, Dalits, and small farmers who call this land home, these sounds have not signaled development—they have heralded displacement.

This book begins with a paradox that defines much of contemporary India: how can a nation aspire to be a global economic powerhouse while displacing millions from their homes, livelihoods, and cultures in the name of that very aspiration? *Displaced by Development* was born from this tension, from years of witnessing, researching, and engaging with the lived experiences of those rendered invisible by bulldozers and balance sheets.

Jharkhand—a state carved from long-standing struggles for tribal autonomy and recognition—embodies the stark contradictions of India's development model. Rich in minerals, it has become a battleground for competing visions of growth and justice. Here, the idea of development has too often been reduced to a story of extraction: of resources from land, of labor from bodies, and of consent from communities. Yet, alongside these forces of dispossession, there exists another story—one of resistance, resilience, and reimagination.

The prologue of this book is not an invitation to view displacement as a distant policy problem or humanitarian crisis. It is a call to see it as a deeply political phenomenon rooted in the structures of state power, corporate capital, and global inequality. It is also an appeal to hear the voices of those who have refused to disappear quietly into the margins, who have asserted their right not only to compensation but to dignity, history, and self-determined futures.

What follows is not a linear account of development or a mere critique of flawed policy. It is a layered exploration—of theories and field realities, of global frameworks and local struggles, of historical injustices and emerging alternatives. It is a book written in solidarity with those whose lives have been dislocated but whose visions of justice remain deeply grounded.

Let us begin, then, not with the promise of development, but with a question that shadows its every claim: when the land is taken, what remains?

INTRODUCTION

Introduction: The Politics of Displacement in India

Development and displacement are deeply intertwined forces that shape the social, economic, and political fabric of India. The post-independence Indian state has consistently pursued rapid economic growth, industrialization, and infrastructural expansion as markers of national progress. However, this pursuit has often come at a significant social cost—most visibly, the large-scale displacement of vulnerable communities, particularly Adivasis (Scheduled Tribes), Dalits, and small farmers. The paradox of India's development trajectory is that while it generates wealth and modernity for some, it simultaneously deepens deprivation, marginalization, and dispossession for others.

Displacement, especially when induced by development, is not merely a physical relocation. It is a profound disruption of lives, livelihoods, cultures, and identities. In India, millions have been uprooted from their ancestral lands for projects such as dams, mines, industrial complexes, highways, and urban expansion. The consequences are not limited to economic loss; they include the erosion of social cohesion, political agency, and cultural continuity. The politics of displacement, therefore, is fundamentally about power—who decides what constitutes development, who benefits from it, and who pays the price.

This introduction sets the stage for a critical examination of the politics of displacement in India, with a particular focus on Jharkhand—a region emblematic of the tensions between resource-rich lands and resource-poor people. It outlines the theoretical frameworks, historical context, and contemporary challenges that define the landscape of development-induced displacement in the country.

1. Historical Context: Development, State Power, and Displacement

Colonial Legacies and the Roots of Dispossession

The roots of displacement in India can be traced to colonial policies that prioritized resource extraction for imperial interests. The British colonial state systematically appropriated forests, minerals, and agricultural land, often dispossessing indigenous and peasant communities. The Permanent Settlement, Forest Acts, and mining concessions laid the groundwork for a developmental paradigm that viewed land and nature primarily as commodities for extraction and profit.

Post-independence, the Indian state inherited and expanded this extractive logic. The rhetoric of nation-building and modernization justified the construction of large dams, steel plants, and mining projects as symbols of progress. Jawaharlal Nehru famously called dams the "temples of modern India," but these temples were built on the displacement of millions, especially in regions like Jharkhand, Chhattisgarh, Odisha, and Andhra Pradesh.

The Nehruvian Model and Its Discontents

The Nehruvian development model, influenced by classical modernization theory, emphasized state-led industrialization, large-scale infrastructure, and planned economic growth. While this model contributed to national integration and economic diversification, it also entrenched patterns of exclusion and marginalization. Displacement was often rationalized as an inevitable sacrifice for the greater good, with little attention to the rights, voices, or rehabilitation of those affected.

The consequences were stark: studies estimate that between 1950 and 2000, over 60 million people were displaced by development projects in India, with Adivasis constituting a disproportionately high share. Rehabilitation policies were often inadequate, poorly implemented, or entirely absent, leading to cycles of impoverishment, landlessness, and social disintegration.

2. Theoretical Foundations: Understanding Development and Displacement

Modernization Theory: Progress and Its Discontents

Modernization theory, dominant in the mid-20th century, conceptualized development as a linear transition from traditional to modern societies. It prioritized economic growth, industrialization, urbanization, and technological advancement as indicators of progress. Displacement, in this framework, was viewed as a temporary disruption—an unfortunate but necessary cost of modernization. The displaced were expected to integrate into the modern economy, often through wage labor or urban migration.

However, modernization theory has been widely critiqued for its ethnocentrism, ahistoricism, and disregard for the agency and aspirations of marginalized communities. Scholars like Arturo Escobar and James Ferguson argue that it imposes Western norms and models onto diverse societies, erasing local histories, cultures, and knowledge systems. In India, the theory's limitations are evident in regions like Jharkhand, where development projects have disrupted not just economies but entire ways of life rooted in land, community, and tradition.

Dependency Theory: Uneven Development and Structural Inequality

Dependency theory emerged as a critique of modernization, emphasizing the exploitative relationships between the "core" (developed countries) and the "periphery" (developing countries). It argued that underdevelopment is not a stage to be overcome, but a condition produced by global capitalism, colonial legacies, and unequal exchange. In this framework, displacement is not accidental but structural—a necessary outcome of resource extraction and accumulation by global and national elites.

Jharkhand exemplifies this dynamic. Its mineral wealth has attracted multinational corporations and state enterprises, but the benefits have largely accrued to outsiders, while local communities bear the costs of environmental degradation, loss of land, and social upheaval. The politics of displacement, therefore, is inseparable from the politics of resource control, class, and caste.

Political Economy Approaches: Power, Capital, and the State

Political economy perspectives foreground the role of power relations, state policies, and capitalist accumulation in shaping patterns of development and displacement. They analyze how the state, in alliance with corporate interests, facilitates the transfer of land and resources from the poor to the rich, often through coercion, legal manipulation, or outright violence. Displacement is thus not a neutral or technical process, but a deeply political one, embedded in struggles over land, identity, and citizenship.

This approach also highlights the agency of displaced communities, who resist, negotiate, and sometimes reshape the terms of development. Movements against dams, mines, and land acquisition—such as the Narmada Bachao Andolan or the struggles in Jharkhand—demonstrate that displacement is a site of contestation, not just victimhood.

Human-Centered and Rights-Based Frameworks

In recent decades, alternative frameworks have emphasized the need for development that expands human capabilities, freedoms, and rights. Amartya Sen's concept of "development as freedom" argues that true progress lies in enhancing people's choices, agency, and well-being, not just in increasing GDP or building infrastructure. Rights-based approaches demand that the voices, consent, and interests of affected communities be central to development planning and implementation.

These perspectives challenge the dominant paradigm by insisting that displacement is not just a logistical issue but a violation of rights, dignity, and justice. They call for policies that prioritize rehabilitation, restitution, and participation, and that recognize the cultural, social, and ecological dimensions of displacement.

3. Jharkhand: A Microcosm of Development and Displacement
Resource Wealth, Human Poverty

Jharkhand is one of India's most resource-rich states, endowed with over 40% of the country's mineral wealth. It has been a focal point for mining, industrialization, and infrastructure projects since colonial times. Yet, paradoxically, Jharkhand ranks low on indicators of health, education, and human development. The wealth extracted from its land has rarely translated into prosperity for its people, especially its Adivasi majority.

The pattern is clear: land and resources are appropriated for "public purpose," but the public that benefits is often distant—urban consumers, industrialists, and state coffers—while the local population is displaced, dispossessed, and marginalized. The politics of displacement in Jharkhand thus encapsulates the broader contradictions of India's development model.

Adivasis and the Struggle for Land and Identity

Adivasis, who constitute a significant proportion of Jharkhand's population, have a deep and symbiotic relationship with their land, forests, and rivers. For them, land is not just an economic asset but a source of identity, spirituality, and community. Displacement severs these bonds, leading not only to economic loss but to cultural and psychological trauma.

Historically, Adivasis have resisted dispossession through a variety of means—legal battles, mass mobilizations, alliances with civil society, and, at times, armed struggle. The creation of Jharkhand as a separate state in 2000 was itself the outcome of decades of agitation for recognition, autonomy, and rights over land and resources. Yet, even after statehood, the pressures of mining, industrialization, and land acquisition have continued unabated, often with the complicity of state institutions.

4. The Politics of Land Acquisition and Rehabilitation

Legal Frameworks and Their Limitations

The legal architecture governing land acquisition in India has evolved over time, but often remains skewed in favor of the state and private capital. The colonial-era Land Acquisition Act of 1894 gave sweeping powers to the state to acquire land for "public purpose," with minimal safeguards for affected communities. Although the Right to Fair Compensation and Transparency in Land Acquisition, Rehabilitation and Resettlement Act (LARR) of 2013 introduced provisions for consent, compensation, and rehabilitation, its implementation has been uneven and contested.

In practice, loopholes, exemptions, and bureaucratic inertia often undermine the spirit of the law. Many projects proceed without genuine consent or adequate rehabilitation, and the definition of "public purpose" is frequently stretched to include private industrial and commercial ventures. The politics of legal reform thus reflects broader struggles over rights, representation, and accountability.

Rehabilitation: Promises and Realities

Rehabilitation and resettlement (R&R) policies are intended to mitigate the adverse impacts of displacement, but their track record in India is mixed at best. Compensation is often delayed, inadequate, or misappropriated. Alternative livelihoods, housing, and social infrastructure are rarely provided in a timely or effective manner. Displaced families frequently end up in informal settlements, facing poverty, insecurity, and social fragmentation.

Moreover, R&R policies tend to focus on individual compensation rather than collective rights, ignoring the communal and cultural dimensions of displacement. The loss of common property resources—forests, grazing lands, water bodies—further undermines the resilience of affected communities.

5. Resistance, Agency, and Alternative Paradigms: Grassroots Movements and the Politics of Resistance

Displacement has generated a vibrant landscape of resistance in India. Movements led by Adivasis, Dalits, farmers, and civil society organizations have challenged the legitimacy of land acquisition, demanded fair compensation, and articulated alternative visions of development. These struggles have taken diverse forms—legal challenges, mass protests, advocacy campaigns, and, in some cases, direct action.

Notable examples include the Narmada Bachao Andolan, the anti-POSCO movement in Odisha, and numerous local struggles in Jharkhand against mining and industrial projects. These movements have not only exposed the injustices of displacement but have also forced the state to reconsider policies, negotiate with affected communities, and, occasionally, halt or modify projects.

Alternative Development Models

The politics of displacement has also spurred debates about alternative models of development. Advocates of sustainable development emphasize the need to balance economic growth with social equity and environmental protection. Community-based resource management, participatory planning, and recognition of customary rights are proposed as ways to ensure that development does not come at the expense of the most vulnerable.

Some states and regions have experimented with models that prioritize local control over resources, equitable benefit-sharing, and environmental sustainability. However, these alternatives face significant challenges from entrenched interests, policy inertia, and the imperatives of global capital.

6. Key Questions and the Way Forward

The politics of displacement in India raises fundamental questions about the meaning and purpose of development:

- Who defines development, and whose interests does it serve?
- Who bears the costs, and who reaps the benefits?
- How can the rights, dignity, and agency of displaced communities be protected and promoted?
- What alternatives exist to the dominant paradigm of extractive, exclusionary development?

Addressing these questions requires more than legal or policy reforms. It demands a transformation of the underlying power structures, a reimagining of development itself, and a commitment to justice, inclusion, and sustainability. The challenge is not just to mitigate the harms of displacement, but to create conditions where development empowers rather than marginalizes, heals rather than divides.

Conclusion: Towards a Just Politics of Development

The story of displacement in India is not just one of loss and suffering; it is also a story of resistance, resilience, and hope. Adivasi and other marginalized communities have consistently asserted their rights, challenged injustice, and articulated alternative visions of development rooted in dignity, autonomy, and sustainability.

The politics of displacement, therefore, is not only about the distribution of resources but about the distribution of power, voice, and recognition. It is about who gets to decide the future of India's land, resources, and people. As India continues to pursue economic growth and modernization, the challenge is to ensure that development does not become a new form of dispossession, but a pathway to justice and empowerment for all.

CHAPTER TWO

Theoretical Foundations of Development and Displacement

India's development journey has always been uneven, often advancing through the marginalisation of its most vulnerable communities. Among them, Scheduled Tribes or Adivasis have been disproportionately affected by state-led industrialisation, infrastructure expansion, and natural resource extraction. Jharkhand serves as a microcosm of this broader pattern.

With over 40% of India's mineral wealth, Jharkhand has long attracted the attention of industrial interests. Yet, despite decades of extractive development, the state ranks low on key indicators of health, education, and human welfare. The cost of this "progress" has been displacement, dispossession, and disempowerment of those least equipped to bear it.

This introductory chapter sets the context for the book, explaining the rationale, objectives, and scope of the inquiry. It outlines the political economy approach, focusing on the intersection of capital, state power, and social structures in shaping displacement. It also introduces the core questions that guide the book: Who benefits from development? Who pays the cost? And what alternatives exist

Development and displacement are deeply intertwined phenomena that shape the social, economic, and political landscape of many regions worldwide. Particularly in developing countries like India, processes of modernization and economic growth have often led to large-scale displacement of vulnerable communities. Understanding the theoretical underpinnings of development is crucial to grasp the complex dynamics that cause displacement and the ensuing socio-political ramifications. This chapter explores key theoretical perspectives on development, including classical and contemporary theories, the conception of development as freedom, and political economy approaches. These frameworks provide a critical lens to analyze displacement as a byproduct of development and highlight the necessity for more inclusive and just development paradigms.

Introduction

Development and displacement are deeply intertwined phenomena that profoundly shape the social, economic, and political fabric of societies across the globe. While development is widely seen as a process aimed at improving human well-being through economic growth, modernization, and infrastructural progress, it often entails significant social costs. One of the most pressing and visible consequences of development, especially in the Global South, is the large-scale displacement of vulnerable communities. This displacement—commonly referred to as development-induced displacement and resettlement (DIDR)—is frequently a byproduct of infrastructure projects such as dams, mining, industrial zones, highways, and urban expansion.

In countries like India, which are characterized by rapid economic transformation alongside entrenched social inequalities, development-induced displacement has emerged as a critical challenge. Millions of people, particularly indigenous tribal groups, peasants, and marginalized communities, are uprooted from their ancestral lands and traditional livelihoods in the name of national progress. This disruption does not simply imply a physical relocation; it often entails the loss of cultural identity, social cohesion, political agency, and economic security. The displaced populations frequently face impoverishment, alienation, and social exclusion, underscoring the paradox of development that generates wealth for some while deepening deprivation for others.

Understanding the complex dynamics between development and displacement requires a robust theoretical framework that goes beyond conventional economic indicators. It calls for an interdisciplinary approach that integrates insights from economics, sociology, political science, anthropology, and human rights perspectives. Theoretical explorations illuminate how different conceptions of development—ranging from growth-centric models to human-centered and rights-based frameworks—shape the policies, practices, and outcomes of development projects.

This chapter undertakes a critical examination of key theoretical perspectives on development, including classical modernization theories, dependency critiques, Amartya Sen's influential idea of development as freedom, and political economy approaches. Each framework offers distinct insights into how development is conceptualized and how displacement is experienced and contested. For instance, classical theories often legitimize displacement as a necessary sacrifice for progress, while human-centric approaches emphasize the expansion of capabilities and freedoms of affected populations. Political economy perspectives, on the other hand, highlight the role of power relations, state policies, and capitalist accumulation in shaping displacement patterns.

By engaging with these theoretical foundations, this chapter aims to provide a nuanced understanding of development-induced displacement. It also seeks to highlight the urgent need for more inclusive, just, and sustainable development paradigms—ones that recognize the rights, dignity, and agency of displaced communities. Such paradigms must strive to reconcile economic growth with social equity and environmental sustainability, ensuring that development becomes a pathway to empowerment rather than marginalization.

Theories of Development

Theories of development offer frameworks to understand how societies grow, transform, and progress across economic, political, social, and cultural dimensions. Rooted in both historical experiences and intellectual traditions, these theories seek to explain the causes of underdevelopment and propose pathways to achieve sustainable and inclusive progress. The concept of "development" itself is contested—while early perspectives focused primarily on economic growth and industrialization, contemporary views emphasize human well-being, social equity, environmental sustainability, and political freedom.

Following the end of World War II, the field of development studies gained prominence, especially in the context of decolonization and the emergence of newly independent nations in Asia, Africa, and Latin America. Scholars and policymakers sought to understand how these countries could "catch up" with the industrialized West. This gave rise to a range of theories, including modernization theory, dependency theory, world-systems theory, neoliberalism, and alternative development paradigms. Each theory reflects a particular worldview—whether optimistic about the universal applicability of Western models or critical of global power structures and inequalities.

In essence, development theories are not only analytical tools but also ideological constructs that shape policy choices, international aid, and institutional strategies. Understanding these theories is crucial for critically engaging with the challenges and possibilities of development in a rapidly changing global order.

Modernization Theory

Modernization theory, dominant in the mid-20th century, views development as a linear process through which traditional societies transform into modern industrial ones (Rostow, 1960). Rooted in Western experiences, it emphasizes economic growth, industrialization, urbanization, and technological progress as key indicators of development. According to this perspective, displacement is often seen as an unfortunate but necessary consequence of modernization, where the greater good of national progress justifies the relocation of marginalized communities (Cernea, 1997).

However, this approach has been criticized for its ethnocentric bias and its failure to consider the socio-cultural dislocations and inequalities generated by such processes (Escobar, 1995). In regions like Jharkhand, this theory inadequately addresses the unique socio-political contexts of tribal communities whose displacement disrupts their livelihoods, social networks, and cultural identities (Xaxa, 1999).

Modernization theory emerged in the aftermath of World War II, during a period when newly independent nations in Asia, Africa, and Latin America were seeking pathways to economic growth and national development. Dominant throughout the 1950s and 1960s, this theory provided a framework for understanding and guiding the transformation of so-called "traditional" societies into "modern" ones. It was closely associated with the Cold War political agenda, as Western nations, particularly the United States, sought to promote capitalist models of development as alternatives to socialism and communism.

W.W. Rostow's *Stages of Economic Growth: A Non-Communist Manifesto* (1960) is one of the most influential formulations of modernization theory. Rostow posited that all societies progress through a series of five stages—from traditional society to the age of mass consumption—driven primarily by industrialization, capital accumulation, and technological innovation. In this schema, development is conceptualized as a linear, universal process where "backward" or "undeveloped" societies are expected to follow the trajectory of the industrialized West.

Modernization theorists emphasized indicators such as Gross Domestic Product (GDP), industrial output, urbanization rates, literacy, and infrastructure development as markers of progress. Within this framework, large-scale projects like dams, highways, factories, and mines were celebrated as signs of advancement and modernization. Displacement resulting from such projects was often viewed as a temporary disruption, a necessary trade-off in the pursuit of national prosperity. The dominant narrative framed displaced populations—often indigenous, rural, or tribal—as obstacles to development who needed to be "integrated" into the modern economy and society.

However, this top-down, technocratic vision of development has faced sustained critique for its ethnocentric, ahistorical, and socially disruptive assumptions. Scholars such as Arturo Escobar (1995) and James Ferguson (1990) have argued that modernization theory imposed Western norms of development onto diverse societies, failing to account for historical injustices, structural inequalities, and local knowledge systems. It neglected the agency, aspirations, and lived realities of the very people it purported to help.

In the Indian context, modernization theory heavily influenced postcolonial state policies, particularly during the Nehruvian era. The Indian state embraced large-scale infrastructure projects such as the Bhakra Nangal Dam and various steel plants as "temples of modern India." However, these projects often led to massive displacement, especially of Adivasi (tribal) populations, without adequate mechanisms for rehabilitation or compensation.

Jharkhand offers a vivid example of the limitations of modernization theory. Rich in natural resources like coal, iron ore, and bauxite, the region became a hotspot for industrial and mining activity post-independence. While such development projects contributed to national economic growth, they simultaneously displaced thousands of tribal families from their ancestral lands. These communities, whose social and cultural lives were intricately linked to their environment, found themselves uprooted and marginalized in unfamiliar urban or peri-urban settings.

The framework of modernization failed to account for the complex relationships tribal people have with their land—not merely as a source of economic sustenance, but as a repository of cultural memory, spiritual significance, and communal identity. The loss of land for them meant the loss of identity, autonomy, and a way of life passed down through generations. The theory's uncritical celebration of growth and industrialization thus obscured the violence and dispossession embedded in the so-called development process.

Moreover, modernization theory offers no adequate tools to understand or respond to the consequences of displacement: social disintegration, psychological trauma, increased poverty, and the erosion of traditional support systems. Its linear and universalist assumptions render invisible the differentiated and uneven impacts of development on various social groups, especially the most vulnerable.

In sum, while classical modernization theory provided a dominant paradigm for post-war development discourse, its relevance in contexts like Jharkhand is highly questionable. By ignoring historical legacies, cultural diversity, and power relations, it contributed to a development model that privileges the interests of elites and corporations over those of marginalized communities. As such, any critical engagement with development-induced displacement must move beyond the narrow confines of modernization and adopt more inclusive and context-sensitive frameworks.

Dependency Theory and Critiques of Development

Emerging as a critical response to modernization theory, dependency theory highlights how development in some countries is intrinsically linked to underdevelopment in others through exploitative global economic structures (Frank, 1967). It emphasizes the role of external forces such as colonial legacies, multinational corporations, and international financial institutions in shaping uneven development patterns.

From this viewpoint, displacement caused by large-scale development projects—such as mining, dams, and industrial zones—can be seen as a manifestation of these structural inequalities, where the local poor bear disproportionate costs for the benefit of national elites and global capital (Baviskar, 1995).

In response to the limitations and ethnocentrism of modernization theory, a powerful body of thought emerged in the 1960s and 1970s, particularly from scholars in Latin America, known as Dependency Theory. This approach fundamentally questioned the linear and universal model of development proposed by modernization theorists and argued that underdevelopment in the Global South was not a stage to be overcome, but rather a condition actively produced by the global capitalist system.

Dependency theorists such as Andre Gunder Frank (1967), Raúl Prebisch, Samir Amin, and Fernando Henrique Cardoso asserted that the historical relationship between the "core" (developed capitalist countries) and the "periphery" (developing or underdeveloped nations) was one of exploitation, not mutual progress. According to this view, the wealth and industrial prosperity of the core were achieved through centuries of colonial plunder, unequal trade, and the continuous extraction of raw materials and labor from the periphery.

This structuralist perspective redefined development not as a neutral process of growth and modernization, but as a political-economic arrangement in which the global South is systematically subordinated to the needs of the global North. In this system, multinational corporations, international financial institutions (like the IMF and World Bank), and elite national governments function together to maintain unequal relations of exchange and accumulation.

Displacement as Structural Violence

From the vantage point of dependency theory, displacement is not merely an accidental consequence of development, but a structural necessity of the global capitalist system. Natural resources—minerals, forests, land—located in the peripheries are extracted for industrial use and profit accumulation in global centers, often with the complicity of national governments and local elites.

In India, and particularly in mineral-rich states like Jharkhand, this critique is strikingly relevant. Jharkhand, with its vast reserves of coal, bauxite, iron ore, and uranium, has been a focal point of extractive development since colonial times. Post-independence, the Indian state adopted a developmental model heavily reliant on resource extraction, with little regard for the rights and interests of the indigenous Adivasi communities who inhabit these lands.

Under this model, mining projects, steel plants, power stations, and industrial corridors have led to the systematic dispossession of tribal populations. These projects are often justified in the name of national interest or economic growth, but the benefits accrue disproportionately to industrial capitalists, urban consumers, and international investors. The costs, meanwhile, are borne by those least equipped to resist—the displaced Adivasis who lose not just land, but also culture, social networks, and livelihoods.

Dependency theorists would interpret such patterns of displacement as instances of "accumulation by dispossession" (a concept later developed by David Harvey), where the resources and labor of the marginalized are expropriated to fuel capitalist growth. Moreover, the flow of surplus value from local communities to urban centers or international markets underscores the ongoing economic dependency of the periphery.

Critique of National Development Models

Dependency theory also critiques the role of the postcolonial state in perpetuating inequalities. Although often portrayed as a benevolent actor, the state can function as an enabler of capitalist interests, prioritizing economic growth over social justice. In India, successive governments have championed mega-projects and foreign investment, frequently overriding local opposition and violating constitutional protections such as the Fifth Schedule (which safeguards tribal areas) and the Panchayats (Extension to Scheduled Areas) Act, 1996 (PESA).

In Jharkhand, for example, numerous movements have emerged—such as the anti-displacement struggle against the Koel-Karo dam, or protests against mining projects in areas like Saranda and Netarhat—challenging the legitimacy of state-sanctioned development that leads to displacement. These movements reflect a growing awareness that development, as currently practiced, is not a neutral or universal good, but often serves to deepen historical inequalities and marginalization.

Broader Critical Perspectives: Escobar and post-development

The critiques launched by dependency theorists were further expanded in the 1980s and 1990s by scholars associated with the post-development school, such as Arturo Escobar (1995) and James Ferguson. Escobar, in particular, argued that "development" itself is a discursive construct imposed on the Global South by Western institutions, framing certain societies as "underdeveloped" in order to legitimize intervention and control. He highlights how development projects often ignore local knowledge systems, traditional economies, and alternative ways of living, imposing instead a universalizing model of progress that leads to cultural homogenization and ecological destruction.

In this framework, displacement is not only material but epistemic—a form of cultural and cognitive colonization that undermines indigenous worldviews and imposes dominant models of economy and governance. In the case of Jharkhand, the imposition of industrial and market logic on Adivasi communities represents not just the loss of land, but the erosion of an entire way of life grounded in communitarian ethics, subsistence farming, and deep spiritual ties to nature.

Dependency theory and its successors offer a radical critique of conventional development paradigms by exposing the global and local power structures that underlie economic growth and resource extraction. In contrast to the optimistic narrative of modernization theory, dependency perspectives reveal development-induced displacement as a manifestation of historical exploitation, neocolonial dependency, and structural inequality.

By applying this lens to contexts such as Jharkhand, it becomes clear that addressing displacement requires more than just improved compensation or resettlement. It demands a fundamental rethinking of development itself—its purposes, beneficiaries, and guiding principles. Without such a shift, displacement will remain a recurring and normalized feature of a development model that privileges profits over people, and growth over justice.

Development as Freedom: A Human-Centric Approach

Amartya Sen's seminal work on *Development as Freedom* (1999) shifted the focus from purely economic growth to expanding the real freedoms that people enjoy. Sen argues that development should be assessed by people's capability to live the kind of life they value, encompassing political freedoms, economic opportunities, social guarantees, and protective security.

This framework is particularly relevant in understanding displacement, as forced relocation often entails the loss of freedoms—freedom of residence, access to natural resources, cultural autonomy, and political voice. In Jharkhand, tribal communities' displacement disrupts their ability to sustain livelihoods, undermines their social fabric, and marginalizes them from decision-making processes affecting their lives (Sundar, 2009).

Development as freedom thus demands a participatory, rights-based approach that centers the agency of affected communities, ensuring that development enhances rather than diminishes their capabilities.

A transformative departure from growth-centric and structuralist development theories came with the work of Amartya Sen, particularly through his seminal book *Development as Freedom* (1999). Sen redefined development not merely as an increase in GDP or industrialization but as the expansion of human capabilities and freedoms. According to Sen, the ultimate aim of development should be to enable individuals to live lives they have reason to value, through the removal of various forms of unfreedom—such as poverty, illiteracy, social exclusion, poor health, and lack of political voice.

Capabilities Approach: A Human-Centric Framework

Sen's capability approach shifts the focus from material resources and economic growth to what people are actually able to do and be—their "functionings" and "capabilities." This framework emphasizes:

- Freedom from deprivation (such as hunger, disease, lack of education).
- Freedom to choose a life path, including cultural, occupational, and community affiliations.
- Agency, or the ability to act and make choices within one's environment.

This perspective allows for a much more pluralistic and inclusive understanding of development, one that recognizes the diversity of human aspirations and social arrangements. In contrast to the deterministic logic of modernization or the structural fatalism of dependency theory, Sen's approach affirms the agency of individuals and communities in shaping their own destinies.

Relevance to Displacement: A Critical Reframing

Within the framework of "development as freedom," displacement represents a severe curtailment of fundamental freedoms. It impairs not only the economic well-being of individuals but also their capabilities to participate in their social and cultural worlds. When communities are forcibly displaced—often without prior informed consent, adequate compensation, or meaningful rehabilitation—they are deprived of:

- The freedom to maintain livelihood through traditional occupations like agriculture, forest gathering, or pastoralism.
- The freedom to participate in cultural and religious practices tied to ancestral lands and local ecosystems.
- The freedom to exercise political agency, as displacement often marginalizes people from decision-making processes and governance institutions.

In Jharkhand, for example, tribal communities derive not only economic sustenance but also social identity, spiritual meaning, and cultural continuity from their lands. Displacement, in this context, is not just a physical relocation; it is an existential rupture that undermines the community's entire way of life. From Sen's perspective, such a process cannot be called development, because it actively reduces the capabilities and freedoms of the people affected.

Expanding the Notion of Justice in Development

Sen's approach also invites a broader normative engagement with justice in development policy. He argues that development must be evaluated based on its actual impact on people's lives and freedoms, not on abstract metrics or top-down objectives. This entails:

- Participatory decision-making: Local communities must be empowered to shape the development processes that affect them.
- Democratic deliberation: Development choices should be open to public reasoning and scrutiny, not imposed through bureaucratic or corporate fiat.
- Recognition of diversity: Cultural, ecological, and social diversity should be seen as assets to development, not obstacles.

In regions like Jharkhand, the implementation of Sen's ideas would mean recognizing tribal ways of life as legitimate and valuable alternatives to industrial development. It would involve a rights-based approach to development, where displacement cannot occur without free, prior, and informed consent (as enshrined in international instruments like the UN Declaration on the Rights of Indigenous Peoples) and where rehabilitation is aimed at restoring or enhancing capabilities, not merely compensating for land loss.

Institutional Applications and Policy Implications

Sen's work has influenced various development policies globally and in India. The Human Development Index (HDI), developed in collaboration with Mahbub ul Haq, incorporates indicators beyond income—such as health and education—to assess national development. Similarly, India's Scheduled Tribes and Other Traditional Forest Dwellers (Recognition of Forest Rights) Act, 2006 (FRA) and Panchayats (Extension to Scheduled Areas) Act, 1996 (PESA) echo elements of capability and freedom, at least in principle.

However, the gap between legislative intent and actual practice remains wide. Many development projects continue to bypass or violate these provisions, treating displacement as a logistical problem rather than a fundamental human rights issue. Applying Sen's framework would require rethinking the goals, methods, and ethics of development to ensure that it expands, rather than erodes, the freedoms of the most marginalized.

Amartya Sen's "Development as Freedom" offers a compelling ethical and practical critique of displacement-centric development. By placing individual and collective freedom at the heart of the development process, Sen challenges the legitimacy of any project that displaces people without enhancing their well-being or agency. In contrast to modernization's technocratic vision and dependency theory's structural determinism, the capabilities approach foregrounds justice, dignity, and participatory inclusion.

Applied to Jharkhand and similar contexts, this perspective demands a paradigm shift—from measuring development by how much land is acquired or capital invested, to how many lives are empowered and freedoms expanded. It is a call for development that is not merely for the people, but by and with the people most affected by it.

Political Economy Approach to Development and Displacement

The political economy approach situates development and displacement within the broader power relations and economic structures of society. It emphasizes how policies, institutions, and economic interests shape who benefits from development and who suffers its costs.

The Political Economy Approach to development and displacement offers a critical framework for understanding how power, capital, and state interests interact to produce patterns of inequality and dispossession. Unlike modernization theory, which focuses on technical progress, or Sen's capability approach, which centers on individual freedoms, political economy foregrounds structural power relations, class dynamics, and the role of the state in shaping who benefits from development—and at whose cost.

At its core, the political economy perspective examines development as a contested process, where different groups—corporations, states, elites, and marginalized communities—vie for control over resources, decision-making, and the direction of change. Displacement, from this viewpoint, is not an unfortunate byproduct of development but often a deliberate outcome of economic strategies designed to favor capital accumulation and elite interests.

Development as Accumulation by Dispossession

A key contribution to this perspective comes from David Harvey's concept of "accumulation by dispossession" (2003), which builds on Karl Marx's notion of "primitive accumulation." Harvey argues that in late capitalism, development often entails the appropriation of common property and public assets—land, water, forests, minerals—for private profit. This process involves coercive legal, institutional, and often violent mechanisms that strip marginalized communities of their resources in order to serve the interests of corporations and the state.

In the context of Jharkhand, the political economy of development is marked by precisely such dynamics. The region, rich in natural resources, has long been targeted for extractive industries such as coal mining, iron ore extraction, power generation, and large-scale industrial projects. These ventures are often promoted under the rhetoric of national development, employment generation, and regional growth. However, a closer examination reveals that:

- The benefits of these projects are disproportionately captured by private companies, state-owned enterprises, and urban elites.
- The costs—land loss, ecological degradation, social fragmentation—are borne almost entirely by tribal and rural communities.
- Displacement is often enabled by legal instruments such as the Land Acquisition Act, or bypassed through state emergency powers, leading to the weakening of democratic safeguards like consent, consultation, and rehabilitation.

The Role of the State

The political economy approach critically analyzes the role of the state not as a neutral arbiter of development but as an active agent in resource extraction and population management. The state is seen as deeply entangled with capital, using its institutional and coercive apparatus—laws, police, bureaucracy—to facilitate the transfer of resources from the margins to the center.

In Jharkhand, the state often functions as a broker between corporate interests and local populations, enabling land acquisition through promises of compensation, employment, and rehabilitation. Yet in practice, rehabilitation policies are frequently underfunded, poorly implemented, or entirely symbolic, leaving displaced families in worsening conditions. This gap between promise and delivery reflects not only bureaucratic inefficiency but also a deeper political logic: the marginalization of those whose existence is seen as an impediment to capital expansion.

Class, Caste, and Capital

The political economy lens also intersects with caste and class analysis, especially in a society like India where social stratification plays a decisive role in access to resources and political power. In Jharkhand, Adivasi communities are not only economically poor but also politically weak, often excluded from formal decision-making processes. Their land is devalued because it is communally held and often lacks formal legal titles, making it more vulnerable to appropriation.

At the same time, local elites—contractors, middlemen, political leaders—frequently act as intermediaries, benefiting from compensation schemes or aligning with outside investors, while the broader community bears the brunt of displacement. This intra-regional inequality deepens the fracture lines within affected communities and often weakens collective resistance to displacement.

Resistance and Counter-Narratives

One of the key strengths of the political economy approach is its attention to resistance movements and counter-hegemonic struggles. In Jharkhand, numerous people's movements have arisen to contest displacement and assert alternative visions of development—movements like those against the Koel-Karo dam, the Netarhat Field Firing Range, or industrial projects in Bokaro, Hazaribagh, and Saranda forests.

These movements are not simply oppositional; they often articulate alternative paradigms of development based on sustainability, community control, and ecological balance. They call for a recognition of customary land rights, environmental justice, and democratic participation in development planning. Viewed through the political economy lens, such movements represent a struggle not only for land but for autonomy, recognition, and self-determination in the face of capitalist and statist expansion.

The Political Economy Approach reveals that displacement is not a marginal or accidental issue but a structural feature of capital-driven development. It exposes the concentration of power and profit, the complicity of the state, and the systemic neglect of marginalized communities. It demands that we look beyond technocratic solutions or moral appeals, and instead confront the institutional and ideological foundations of dispossession.

In the context of Jharkhand, this perspective helps us see development-induced displacement as a symptom of deeper contradictions between extractive economic growth and social justice. Any meaningful response to displacement must therefore go beyond compensation and focus on redistribution of power, recognition of rights, and restructuring of developmental priorities in favor of those most affected.

Power, Inequality, and Displacement

Displacement is rarely a neutral event; it reflects the struggles over resources and control between powerful actors—state agencies, corporations, political elites—and marginalized populations. In Jharkhand, the political economy of displacement is shaped by:

- The state's role in facilitating resource extraction and infrastructural projects often aligned with corporate interests (Mahapatra & Mishra, 2018).
- The marginalization of tribal land rights under legal frameworks such as the Land Acquisition Act and inadequate implementation of the Forest Rights Act (2006) (Padel & Das, 2010).
- The socio-economic vulnerability of displaced communities, who often lack adequate compensation or rehabilitation, leading to impoverishment and social disintegration (Cernea, 1997; Baviskar, 2004).

Development-Induced Displacement as Political Economy

From this perspective, displacement is understood not just as an outcome of development but as a process embedded in capitalist accumulation and state governance. It exposes contradictions in development policies, where economic growth objectives clash with social justice and environmental sustainability (Harvey, 2005).

The political economy lens demands critical scrutiny of displacement policies and calls for redistributive measures, stronger legal protections for indigenous lands, and democratization of decision-making to empower displaced communities (D'Costa, 2011).

Displacement is not merely an unfortunate byproduct of development; rather, from a political economy perspective, it is a structured and systemic outcome of economic and political processes designed to facilitate capital accumulation, often at the cost of marginalized communities. This framework situates development-induced displacement within the broader dynamics of capitalist expansion, state intervention, and class/caste hierarchies, highlighting how development projects—dams, mines, infrastructure, industrial zones—serve not only developmental objectives but also the interests of economic and political elites.

Displacement and Capitalist Accumulation

Drawing on David Harvey's (2005) concept of "accumulation by dispossession," displacement is understood as a contemporary form of primitive accumulation, wherein land, forests, water, and other communal resources are forcibly appropriated from the poor and transferred to private or state control for capital investment. In this sense, development becomes a mechanism of expropriation, in which the livelihoods and socio-cultural fabrics of rural and tribal populations are dismantled to make way for urban-industrial expansion.

In Jharkhand, such dynamics are visibly present. The region's mineral wealth—coal, iron ore, bauxite, uranium—has attracted multinational corporations and public sector enterprises. Under the guise of "public interest" or "national development," vast tracts of tribal land have been acquired for mining, power plants, steel factories, and other mega-projects. However, these projects often fail to benefit the displaced populations. Instead:

- Livelihoods are disrupted, as land-based economies are replaced with precarious wage labor or unemployment.
- Social cohesion is eroded, as communities are scattered and relocated without adequate planning.
- Cultural and spiritual ties to land are broken, particularly for indigenous groups who view land not merely as property but as identity and ancestry.
- Environmental degradation ensues, leading to deforestation, water pollution, and loss of biodiversity.

Thus, displacement is not incidental but structurally built into the logic of capitalist development, whereby land becomes a commodity and local populations are seen as obstacles to economic growth.

The Role of the State: Facilitator of Dispossession

The political economy lens also emphasizes the active role of the state in enabling displacement. Far from being a neutral actor, the state often acts as a broker for corporate capital, using its legal, bureaucratic, and coercive apparatus to acquire land, suppress resistance, and justify development narratives. Laws like the Land Acquisition Act (1894, and later 2013) and policies under Special Economic Zones (SEZs) have been used to override local customary rights and community consent.

In tribal regions of Jharkhand, despite constitutional protections under the Fifth Schedule, the Panchayats (Extension to Scheduled Areas) Act, 1996 (PESA), and the Forest Rights Act, 2006 (FRA), large-scale displacement continues unabated. These legal frameworks, while progressive on paper, are often ignored or manipulated to serve the interests of extractive industries. State authorities frequently undermine traditional governance institutions such as Gram Sabhas and fail to implement free, prior, and informed consent as mandated by both national and international legal norms (e.g., UNDRIP).

This convergence of state and capital interest leads to a phenomenon that Partha Chatterjee terms the "political society"—where marginalized groups exist outside the realm of rights-bearing citizens and are instead governed through exceptional measures, welfare promises, or outright force.

Contradictions in Development Policy

The political economy approach helps expose the inherent contradictions in mainstream development policy:

- On one hand, the state commits to inclusive growth, tribal welfare, environmental protection, and participatory democracy.
- On the other hand, its actions facilitate resource extraction, forced displacement, ecological destruction, and disempowerment of the poor.

This contradiction reflects what Duncan Green (2008) describes as a "double discourse" of development—where policy rhetoric speaks of equity and justice, but practice is shaped by the imperatives of capital and state control. In this duality, displaced populations become invisible or sacrificial, often denied not only compensation and rehabilitation but also recognition and voice.

Toward a Radical Policy Shift: Redistributive and Democratic Imperatives

The political economy approach does not merely diagnose problems—it demands systemic alternatives. As D'Costa (2011) and other scholars argue, resolving the crisis of displacement requires a restructuring of development priorities and power relations. Key imperatives include:

- Redistributive justice: Ensuring that the gains of development are shared equitably and that affected communities are not just compensated but recompensed in a manner that restores dignity, autonomy, and livelihood.
- Legal empowerment: Strengthening legal protections for indigenous and forest-dwelling communities through strict enforcement of laws like FRA and PESA, recognition of customary tenure, and removal of bureaucratic obstacles in securing land titles.
- Democratization of development planning: Moving away from technocratic, top-down models to community-led development, where displaced people are not passive recipients of aid but active decision-makers in the planning, execution, and monitoring of projects.
- Environmental sustainability: Reimagining development in a way that respects ecological limits, preserves biodiversity, and values traditional knowledge systems that promote conservation.

Furthermore, development-induced displacement must be placed within the broader struggle for social transformation, wherein capitalist modes of production and state structures are interrogated, and alternative paradigms—such as eco-socialism, solidarity economies, or degrowth—are considered as viable paths toward justice.

Viewed through the political economy lens, development-induced displacement is a deeply political and structural phenomenon, embedded in the dynamics of capitalist accumulation, state power, and social exclusion. In this framework, displacement is not an anomaly but a predictable and systemic outcome of development strategies that prioritize profit over people, growth over equity, and control over consent.

In regions like Jharkhand, where resource wealth coexists with widespread poverty and marginalization, this analysis helps uncover the real costs of development—not just in terms of GDP loss or rehabilitation failure, but in the loss of community, culture, ecology, and autonomy.

To move beyond this crisis, the political economy approach calls for a radical rethinking of development: one that redistributes power and resources, restores rights and recognition, and re-centers the voices of those who have been historically displaced—not just from their lands, but from the very imagination of development itself.

Case Examples from Jharkhand

Mining and Displacement in Jharkhand

Jharkhand, rich in mineral resources, has witnessed large-scale displacement due to mining projects by both government and private actors. The expansion of coal mining in areas like East Singhbhum and Dhanbad districts has displaced numerous tribal communities without adequate rehabilitation (Mahapatra & Mishra, 2018). The loss of forest land and traditional commons has severed indigenous peoples' link to their ancestral livelihoods, exacerbating poverty and social marginalization (Padel & Das, 2010).

Dam Projects and Tribal Displacement

The construction of dams such as the Subernarekha and the Koel-Karo projects has resulted in significant tribal displacement in Jharkhand (Sundar, 2009). Despite promises of development and resettlement, many displaced families remain landless and impoverished. The displacement also disrupts cultural practices and community cohesion, highlighting the insufficiency of compensation schemes that do not account for socio-cultural losses.

Here is an expanded and elaborated version of Section 4: Case Examples from Jharkhand, integrating field insights, scholarly analysis, and policy critique to deepen the discussion on development-induced displacement:

The state of Jharkhand serves as a compelling case study in understanding the lived realities of development-induced displacement (DID) through the lens of political economy. Known for its abundant natural resources—coal, iron ore, bauxite, and uranium—Jharkhand has become a hub for extractive industries, infrastructure development, and large-scale public sector projects. However, these processes have disproportionately affected Adivasi (indigenous) and other marginalized communities, who have borne the brunt of displacement while receiving limited, if any, benefits from the resulting development.

Displacement in Jharkhand is not just a question of physical relocation; it represents a rupture in socio-economic structures, cultural traditions, and ecological balances. It highlights the disconnect between state-led development narratives and ground-level experiences of dispossession, especially among vulnerable communities.

Mining and Displacement in Jharkhand

Mining is one of the most significant drivers of displacement in Jharkhand. The coalfields of Dhanbad, Bokaro, Hazaribagh, and East

Singhbhum have seen extensive displacement of Adivasi and Dalit communities over decades. Both public sector undertakings like Coal India Limited and private corporations have been involved in acquiring large tracts of land—often forested or communally owned—for mining operations.

According to Mahapatra and Mishra (2018), these mining projects have displaced thousands of families, with rehabilitation policies remaining grossly inadequate. Land acquisition often occurs without proper consent or community consultation, violating the provisions of PESA and the Forest Rights Act (FRA). Once displaced, families are rarely provided with equivalent land, sustainable livelihoods, or access to basic services such as health, education, and water.

Furthermore, mining-related displacement is not just economic—it is ecological and cultural. As Padel and Das (2010) emphasize, forest lands in tribal areas are not merely economic resources but are central to Adivasi identity, spirituality, and social systems. Mining leads to:

- Deforestation and environmental degradation, including contamination of water bodies and depletion of groundwater.
- Air and noise pollution, which has public health consequences.
- Loss of traditional commons, including grazing areas, minor forest produce zones, and sacred groves.
- Erosion of collective ownership systems, as customary land tenure is often not recognized by the state.

Moreover, the employment generated by mining is limited, often contractual and exploitative, with local people replaced by migrant laborers. As a result, mining displaces not only people but entire ways of life, pushing communities into cycles of poverty, dependency, and social fragmentation.

Large-scale dam construction has been another significant cause of displacement in Jharkhand. The Subernarekha Multipurpose Project, initiated in the 1970s and affecting areas in East Singhbhum and Seraikela-Kharsawan districts, led to the displacement of thousands of Adivasi families. Similarly, the Koel-Karo hydroelectric project, proposed in the 1970s and later revived multiple times, became a major flashpoint in the history of tribal resistance in India.

As Sundar (2009) documents, the affected tribal communities vehemently opposed the Koel-Karo project, citing lack of proper consultation, threats to their sacred sites, and fears of cultural extinction. The project would have submerged over 100 villages and more than 150 religious and cultural sites, including Sarna and Masna sacred groves central to Adivasi religion and customs.

Although both projects were justified by the state in terms of power generation, irrigation, and regional development, the actual human and ecological costs far outweighed the projected benefits for local populations:

- Compensation packages were minimal, delayed, or mismanaged, often excluding women and those without formal land titles.
- Resettlement colonies lacked basic infrastructure, such as roads, schools, and drinking water.
- Livelihood restoration was nonexistent, forcing displaced persons into wage labor, migration, or destitution.
- Social disintegration followed, as communities were split up, elders lost traditional authority, and youth became alienated from ancestral heritage.

The displacement caused by these dam projects underscores a critical flaw in mainstream development policy: failure to recognize the intangible, non-economic losses suffered by displaced people. Cultural practices, oral traditions, inter-generational knowledge, and sacred landscapes are irreplaceable, yet they are routinely excluded from cost-benefit calculations.

The Koel-Karo movement, sustained over decades and led largely by tribal women and elders, eventually forced the state to halt the project. This rare instance of successful resistance illustrates both the deep attachment of Adivasi communities to their land and culture, and the possibilities of collective mobilization in the face of development aggression.

Institutional Responses and the Rehabilitation Crisis

While the Jharkhand government and central authorities have framed rehabilitation and resettlement (R&R) policies, their implementation has been deeply flawed. The National Rehabilitation and Resettlement Policy (2007) and Jharkhand's state-level policies often focus narrowly on monetary compensation rather than ensuring a comprehensive recovery of livelihood, social dignity, and cultural continuity.

Field studies reveal several structural challenges:

- Lack of updated land records and unclear ownership patterns hinder fair compensation.
- Absence of gender-sensitive policies results in women losing access to land and decision-making.
- Corruption and bureaucratic red tape delay rehabilitation efforts.
- Fragmentation of affected families, as members move to different locations for work, disrupts community solidarity.

Thus, the rehabilitation process often replicates the very marginalization it claims to redress, making displacement not a one-time event but a prolonged condition of precarity and exclusion.

The experience of mining and dam-related displacement in Jharkhand provides crucial empirical grounding for the theoretical insights discussed earlier in this chapter. These case studies illustrate how development projects, driven by capitalist and statist imperatives, systematically displace marginalized communities, stripping them not just of land but of dignity, culture, and ecological security. The state, instead of acting as a guardian of rights, often facilitates such dispossession under the rhetoric of progress and national interest.

These cases underscore the need for a radical shift in how development is conceptualized and practiced—from being extractive and top-down to being participatory, inclusive, and ecologically sustainable. They also point to the importance of recognizing the agency of displaced communities, not just as victims, but as resistors, negotiators, and claimants of alternative futures.

Conclusion: Rethinking Development and Displacement

The theoretical foundations of development reveal a spectrum of perspectives that range from growth-centric modernization models to more nuanced human-centric and political economy approaches. Recognizing displacement as an inherent yet contested dimension of development challenges simplistic narratives of progress and highlights the need for alternative frameworks.

In regions like Jharkhand, where tribal communities face repeated displacement, these theories underscore the urgency of reimagining development to be inclusive, just, and empowering. Only by centering the freedoms, rights, and voices of displaced peoples can development truly serve as a pathway to human flourishing rather than marginalization.

The phenomenon of development-induced displacement represents one of the most critical contradictions in the contemporary development discourse. As this chapter has explored, displacement is not an accidental or unforeseen outcome of development—it is often an inherent and systemic product of the ways in which development is theorized, planned, and implemented.

From the vantage point of classical modernization theory, displacement is rationalized as a temporary sacrifice in the pursuit of national progress, industrial growth, and modernization. This perspective, however, fails to account for the deep socio-cultural and economic ruptures experienced by displaced populations, especially indigenous communities whose life-worlds are intimately tied to land, forest, and local ecologies.

Amartya Sen's "Development as Freedom" offers a more human-centered alternative, stressing the importance of expanding people's capabilities and freedoms. Yet even this approach often falls short in practice when structural inequalities and power asymmetries are ignored. In contexts like Jharkhand, where land alienation and social marginalization are entrenched, development cannot be equated with mere service delivery or economic opportunity. It must address historical injustices and enable real participation by affected communities.

The political economy perspective brings a sharper critical lens, revealing how development is shaped by the imperatives of capital accumulation, elite interests, and state power. Displacement, in this view, is not a deviation but a deliberate restructuring of space and society in favor of economic and political elites. This approach helps expose the stark inequalities embedded in development practices and underscores the need for redistributive justice, legal empowerment, and democratic governance.

The case studies from Jharkhand—including displacement due to mining in Dhanbad and East Singhbhum, and dam projects like Subernarekha and Koel-Karo—offer a sobering glimpse into how these theoretical concerns materialize on the ground. Despite the promises of progress and rehabilitation, the lived reality for most displaced communities is one of dispossession, impoverishment, and cultural erosion. These examples also reveal the limitations of existing policies and legal frameworks, which often fail to protect vulnerable populations or to deliver meaningful restitution.

What emerges, then, is an urgent need to redefine the very meaning and practice of development. A just and inclusive development paradigm must go beyond the rhetoric of GDP growth and infrastructure expansion.

It must:

- Recognize the rights of indigenous and marginalized communities as central—not peripheral—to development.
- Respect local knowledge systems, cultures, and ecological relationships, treating them not as obstacles but as resources for sustainable development.
- Ensure genuine participation and consent in all stages of project planning and execution, empowering local governance institutions such as Gram Sabhas.
- Implement robust legal safeguards and ensure that compensation and rehabilitation policies are not just financial but socio-culturally sensitive.
- Shift from extractivism to sustainability, focusing on models of development that balance human needs with environmental stewardship.

In essence, the chapter calls for a paradigm shift—from development that displaces, disenfranchises, and divides, to development that dignifies, democratizes, and distributes. Only through such a shift can we begin to reconcile the goals of economic progress with the imperatives of social justice and ecological sustainability.

The case of Jharkhand, while regionally specific, holds broader lessons for India and the Global South. It challenges us to ask: *Whose development? At what cost? And for whose benefit?* Addressing these questions is not just an academic or policy exercise—it is a moral and political necessity.

CHAPTER THREE

UNDERSTANDING DEVELOPMENT-INDUCED DISPLACEMENT

Understanding development-induced displacement requires grounding in multiple theoretical perspectives that interrogate the meaning, purpose, and consequences of development. This chapter explores the intellectual foundations of development thought, drawing from classical development theories, the Capability Approach of Amartya Sen, and the political economy critique of mainstream development paradigms.

Understanding development-induced displacement (DID) requires a comprehensive exploration of the ideological, theoretical, and structural foundations of development. Displacement is not merely a logistical consequence of infrastructural expansion or economic modernization—it is deeply embedded in how development is conceptualized, justified, and operationalized. This chapter seeks to unpack the intellectual and normative assumptions underlying development practices, with the aim of better understanding the systemic nature of displacement.

To do so, the chapter is structured around three key theoretical frameworks:

1. Classical development theories, which provide the foundational narratives of modernization and progress.
2. Amartya Sen's Capability Approach, which redefines development in terms of human freedom and well-being.
3. The political economy critique, which interrogates the structural inequalities, power relations, and capitalist imperatives that drive

displacement.

Through this tripartite framework, the chapter analyzes how different models of development explain (or obscure) the causes and consequences of displacement, especially among vulnerable and marginalized populations in contexts like Jharkhand.

Classical Development Theories and the Displacement Paradigm

Classical development theories, especially those emerging in the post-World War II era, viewed development primarily through the lens of economic growth, industrialization, and technological modernization. Rooted in Western historical experiences, these theories posited a linear model of transformation from 'traditional' to 'modern' societies.

Modernization Theory and Linear Progress

The most influential among these is Rostow's "Stages of Economic Growth" (1960), which outlined a sequence of developmental stages culminating in a state of high mass consumption. According to this model, societies must undergo structural transformation—urbanization, mechanization, and bureaucratic rationalization—to achieve prosperity.

In this framework, displacement is not considered a fundamental problem but a necessary byproduct of progress. Land acquisition for infrastructure, mining, or dams is often justified as part of the 'take-off' stage, where sacrifices by some are deemed acceptable for the greater good of national development.

However, such perspectives have been widely criticized for:

- Ethnocentrism, as they universalize Western development experiences.
- Technocratic bias, where social costs like displacement are minimized or ignored.
- Neglect of local contexts, such as the socio-cultural specificities of tribal and indigenous communities.

In regions like Jharkhand, where land is tied not only to economy but to identity, spirituality, and community, this theory fails to grasp the magnitude of loss incurred through displacement.

2.2 Amartya Sen and the Capability Approach: A Human-Centered View

Reacting to the narrow economic focus of earlier models, Amartya Sen's Capability Approach (1999) redefined development as the expansion of people's freedoms and capabilities. Rather than judging progress solely through GDP growth or industrial output, Sen argued that development must be assessed based on individuals' ability to live lives they value.

Freedom as the Core of Development

For Sen, development should enhance:

- Political freedoms (participation, accountability)
- Economic facilities (access to markets, employment)
- Social opportunities (education, healthcare)
- Transparency guarantees (honest governance)
- Protective security (social safety nets)

Displacement, from this perspective, is not just a physical relocation—it represents a deprivation of basic capabilities: loss of housing, livelihoods, education, health, community ties, and political voice. If development leads to a reduction in these freedoms, it fails the normative criteria of being just or beneficial.

In cases like Jharkhand, displaced tribal communities are often thrust into precarious urban informal economies, cut off from their ecological knowledge systems and cultural institutions. They experience a significant drop in their capability sets, indicating that such displacement contradicts the very essence of development as envisioned by Sen.

Yet, critics of the Capability Approach argue that while it provides a powerful evaluative tool, it does not fully account for structural power dynamics—how and why certain groups are excluded from development benefits or why state and corporate actors prioritize certain forms of development over others. For that, a political economy analysis is essential.

Political Economy of Displacement: Power, Capital, and Inequality

The political economy approach offers a more radical and structural critique of development and displacement. It situates development within the global system of capitalist accumulation, state formation, and class struggle, arguing that development is often a tool used by dominant actors to appropriate land, labor, and natural resources.

Displacement as Accumulation by Dispossession

David Harvey's (2005) concept of "accumulation by dispossession" explains how capitalist expansion requires the expropriation of public or communal goods for private profit—through land grabs, resource extraction, and forced displacement. In this view, development projects are not neutral or benevolent—they are mechanisms through which the state and capital displace the poor to enable accumulation by elites.

In the Indian context, the state plays a dual role: as a facilitator of capital and a legitimizer of development narratives. Displacement is justified in the name of nation-building or modernization, while legal frameworks like the Land Acquisition Act or weak enforcement of Forest Rights enable the mass transfer of land from indigenous communities to corporations.

This framework explains why:

- Displacement disproportionately affects tribal, Dalit, and rural communities.
- Compensation and rehabilitation schemes are systematically underfunded or mismanaged.
- Resistance movements are often criminalized or co-opted by the state.

The political economy critique reveals that displacement is not just a development failure—it is often a development strategy designed to serve the interests of dominant social classes and political regimes.

Toward an Integrated Understanding

Each of the above frameworks offers distinct insights into the problem of development-induced displacement:

- Modernization theory explains the logic behind displacement but normalizes it as inevitable and justified.
- The Capability Approach challenges this logic, emphasizing well-being and dignity, but lacks tools to fully address systemic inequalities.
- The Political Economy Perspective exposes the structural violence and exploitation embedded in development policies but may sometimes underemphasize individual agency or cultural meanings of development.

An integrated understanding of displacement must therefore:

- Recognize the multidimensional losses (economic, social, cultural, psychological) caused by displacement.
- Acknowledge the structural inequalities and institutional biases that reproduce cycles of dispossession.
- Embrace alternative development paradigms, including indigenous worldviews, ecological models, and participatory governance.

Development-induced displacement is a deeply political and contested phenomenon. Theoretical models of development shape how displacement is perceived, justified, and addressed. Whether seen as an unfortunate cost (modernization), a failure of freedom (Sen), or a deliberate strategy of capital (political economy), what remains clear is that displacement represents a profound disruption in the lives of affected communities.

As the next chapter will show through empirical evidence from Jharkhand, these theoretical insights are not abstract—they manifest in the lives, struggles, and resistances of real people. A deeper understanding of DID requires both critical theory and grounded reality, so we may move toward development that is not only materially prosperous but also socially just and ecologically sustainable.

Here is a summary box in infographic-style format to accompany Understanding Development-Induced Displacement, offering a concise reference for the three key theoretical perspectives discussed

Modernization Theory

- Development is a linear path from traditional to modern society - Emphasizes industrialization, urbanization, GDP growth

Displacement is necessary and justified for national progress

- Ethnocentric and Western-centric - Ignores cultural and social losses

Capability Approach (Sen)

- Development = expansion of freedoms and human capabilities - Focuses on well-being, agency, and social justice

Displacement undermines basic capabilities (health, education, livelihood)

- Lacks structural analysis - Does not explain power asymmetries clearly

Political Economy Approach

- Development is shaped by capitalist interests and state power - Emphasizes inequality, exploitation, and dispossession

Displacement is a strategic tool of capital accumulation ("accumulation by dispossession")

- May underemphasize individual/community agency - Can overlook cultural meanings

To fully understand development-induced displacement, we must move beyond narrow economic indicators and embrace critical, multidimensional, and participatory frameworks that prioritize justice, inclusion, and ecological sustainability.

1. Classical Theories of Development

Theories of development historically emphasized linear progress toward modernization. W.W. Rostow's "Stages of Economic Growth" model typified this view, positing that all societies must pass through five stages from traditional to high mass-consumption economies. This framework, however, overlooked the structural constraints and historical injustices faced by postcolonial societies.

Modernization theory assumed a universal path to progress, privileging Western industrial models while marginalizing indigenous systems of knowledge, production, and governance. It did not account for the unequal global structures that inhibit development in the Global South.

2. Dependency and World-Systems Theories

Critiques of modernization emerged in the form of Dependency Theory and World-Systems Theory. Scholars like Andre Gunder Frank and Immanuel Wallerstein argued that underdevelopment is not a natural condition but a consequence of exploitative relationships between the core (developed countries) and the periphery (developing countries).

In the Indian context, dependency theory sheds light on how postcolonial states like Jharkhand, though mineral-rich, remain economically marginalized due to the extractive logic of global capitalism and state policies that privilege external investment over local welfare.

Dependency Theory and World-Systems Theory emerged as critical responses to the optimism of modernization theory. While modernization theorists argued that all societies progress through similar linear stages toward development, dependency and world-systems theorists contended that underdevelopment is not a natural or internal condition, but a result of exploitative global relationships.

Pioneered by scholars like Andre Gunder Frank, dependency theory posits that the global capitalist system is structured to benefit a "core" of wealthy, industrialized nations at the expense of a "periphery" of poorer, resource-rich countries. Frank argued that underdevelopment in the periphery is directly linked to the development of the core, through mechanisms such as:

- Metropolis-Satellite Relationship: Economic surplus flows from peripheral rural areas to urban centers and then to international metropoles, leaving the periphery impoverished.
- Historical Exploitation: Colonialism, imperialism, and ongoing neo-colonial practices have locked peripheral countries into roles as suppliers

of cheap raw materials and labor, while core countries accumulate wealth through manufacturing and finance.
- Structural Dependence: Peripheral countries become dependent on core countries for capital, technology, and markets, resulting in a cycle of debt, capital flight, and economic vulnerability.

Frank rejected the idea that underdevelopment is due to internal factors or a lack of modernization. Instead, he argued that the global capitalist system itself produces and perpetuates underdevelopment, and that genuine progress requires breaking free from these exploitative relationships.

World-Systems Theory

Immanuel Wallerstein expanded on dependency theory with his World-Systems Theory, which conceptualizes the world economy as a single, integrated system divided into core, semi-periphery, and periphery regions. Key features include:

- Core Countries: Industrialized, economically dominant, and exploit peripheral countries for raw materials and labor.
- Peripheral Countries: Provide cheap labor and resources, remain underdeveloped, and are dependent on the core for capital and technology.
- Semi-Periphery: Countries that exhibit characteristics of both core and periphery, sometimes exploiting others while being exploited themselves.
- Mechanisms of Exploitation: The global market redistributes surplus value from the periphery to the core, maintaining and reinforcing global inequalities.

World-systems theory emphasizes that development and underdevelopment are not isolated phenomena but are interconnected and systemic, shaped by global capitalism's hierarchical structure.

The Indian Context: Jharkhand and the Logic of Extraction

In postcolonial India, and especially in resource-rich states like Jharkhand, dependency theory provides a powerful lens to understand persistent underdevelopment despite abundant natural wealth. Jharkhand's mineral resources have attracted significant external investment and state-backed extraction projects. However, instead of fostering local prosperity, these projects often result in:

- Displacement of Indigenous Communities: Large-scale mining and industrial projects displace Adivasi communities, eroding traditional livelihoods and social structures.
- Extraction for External Benefit: The wealth generated from Jharkhand's resources primarily benefits external actors—national corporations, global markets, and metropolitan centers—rather than local populations.
- Perpetuation of Poverty: Despite resource extraction, Jharkhand remains economically marginalized, with high poverty rates and poor human development indicators.
- Policy Bias: State policies frequently privilege external investment and industrialization over the welfare and rights of local communities, reflecting the logic of dependency and world-systems theories.

This dynamic mirrors Frank's argument that underdevelopment is produced through the extraction of surplus from the periphery to the core, and Wallerstein's insight that global capitalism organizes regions into hierarchies of exploitation.

Dependency and world-systems theories reveal that underdevelopment in places like Jharkhand is not a result of isolation or lack of modernization, but a consequence of their integration into a global system designed to extract value for the benefit of others. These frameworks challenge the assumptions of modernization theory and call for a re-examination of development policies that perpetuate dependency and displacement, advocating instead for models that prioritize local welfare, autonomy, and equitable resource distribution.

Development as Freedom: The Capability Approach

Amartya Sen's "Development as Freedom" reframed development not as GDP growth but as the expansion of human capabilities—the substantive freedoms people enjoy to live lives they value. These include political freedoms, social opportunities, economic facilities, transparency guarantees, and protective security.

Sen's framework is particularly relevant to Jharkhand, where development has often eroded rather than enhanced people's capabilities. Displaced Adivasis may receive monetary compensation but lose their freedom to work, learn, participate, and sustain their cultural identities.

Sen's approach underscores the centrality of agency in development. True development must empower people to shape their futures, not reduce them to passive recipients of state interventions or victims of corporate expansion.

Amartya Sen's "Development as Freedom" represents a paradigm shift in thinking about development, moving away from the traditional focus on GDP growth and material wealth to the expansion of human capabilities—the real freedoms people have to lead lives they value. According to Sen, development should be assessed by the substantive choices and opportunities available to individuals, not merely by economic output or income levels.

Core Elements of the Capability Approach

Sen's framework identifies five distinct types of freedoms essential for development:

- Political Freedoms: The ability to participate in political processes, express opinions, and have a voice in governance.
- Economic Facilities: Access to resources, employment, and markets that allow people to earn a livelihood and improve their well-being.
- Social Opportunities: Availability of education, healthcare, and social services that empower individuals to fulfill their potential.
- Transparency Guarantees: Openness and trust in institutions, ensuring that people can interact and transact without fear of corruption or discrimination.
- Protective Security: Social safety nets that protect the vulnerable from extreme deprivation and insecurity[2].

Sen argues that poverty is not just a lack of income, but a deprivation of basic capabilities—such as the ability to be healthy, educated, and participate in community life. Thus, development policy should focus on removing "unfreedoms" that limit people's choices and agency.

Relevance to Jharkhand and Displacement

Sen's capability approach is particularly pertinent to regions like Jharkhand, where large-scale development projects—such as mining, industrialization, and infrastructure—have often resulted in the displacement of Adivasi (indigenous) communities. While these projects may bring monetary compensation, they frequently erode the actual freedoms and capabilities of those displaced:

- Loss of Livelihood: Displaced communities lose access to land, forests, and traditional occupations, undermining their economic security and self-sufficiency.

- Cultural Dislocation: Forced migration disrupts social networks, cultural practices, and community cohesion, leading to a loss of identity and belonging.
- Reduced Agency: Displaced individuals often become passive recipients of state aid or compensation, rather than active participants in shaping their futures.
- Limited Access to Services: Relocation sites may lack adequate education, healthcare, and infrastructure, further constraining the capabilities of affected populations.

Sen's approach underscores that true development must empower people to make meaningful choices and exercise agency over their lives. Simply providing compensation or material benefits is insufficient if people lose the freedom to work, learn, participate in society, and sustain their cultural identities.

Agency and Participatory Development

A central tenet of Sen's philosophy is the importance of agency—the ability of individuals to act and bring about change in their own lives and communities. Development should not reduce people to passive recipients of top-down interventions or victims of market forces. Instead, policies must be designed to expand people's real freedoms and support their capacity to shape their destinies.

In the context of Jharkhand, this means:

- Involving Affected Communities: Ensuring that Adivasis and other marginalized groups have a genuine say in decisions about development projects and resettlement.
- Protecting Cultural Rights: Recognizing and preserving the cultural and social fabric of displaced communities.
- Investing in Capabilities: Providing education, skill development, and healthcare to enhance the capabilities of those affected by displacement.

Amartya Sen's "Development as Freedom" reframes development as the expansion of human capabilities and substantive freedoms, rather than mere economic growth. In regions like Jharkhand, where displacement has often undermined people's agency and well-being, Sen's approach highlights the need for development strategies that prioritize human dignity, empowerment, and participatory decision-making. True development is achieved not by imposing external models, but by enabling people to lead lives they have reason to valu

The Political Economy Approach

The political economy perspective highlights how development is shaped by power, interests, and institutions. It interrogates the beneficiaries and losers of development policies, focusing on class dynamics, state-corporate alliances, and historical structures of dispossession.

Jharkhand exemplifies the asymmetrical nature of development. While corporate actors and political elites benefit from mining and industrial projects, local communities—especially Adivasis—are uprooted, disempowered, and marginalized. Development, in this light, becomes a mode of accumulation by dispossession.

This approach challenges technocratic and apolitical narratives of progress and calls for democratic participation, equitable distribution, and structural transformation in development planning.

The Political Economy Approach: Power, Dispossession, and Development

The political economy approach to development moves beyond purely economic or technocratic explanations and foregrounds the central role of power relations, interests, and institutional frameworks in shaping development outcomes. This perspective critically examines who benefits and who loses from development policies, highlighting the often unequal and contested nature of economic growth and social change.

Power, Interests, and Institutions

At its core, political economy asks:

- Whose interests are served by development projects?
- Who holds the power to make decisions?
- How do institutions—laws, policies, and governance structures—shape the distribution of resources and opportunities?

This approach recognizes that development is not a neutral or universally beneficial process. Instead, it is shaped by the interplay of powerful actors (such as the state, corporations, and global financial institutions) and is deeply embedded in historical and structural inequalities.

Accumulation by Dispossession

Drawing on the work of scholars like David Harvey, the political economy perspective introduces the concept of accumulation by dispossession. This refers to the process by which wealth and resources are concentrated in the hands of a few through the dispossession and marginalization of others. In the context of Jharkhand:

- Corporate and Elite Gains: Mining, industrial, and infrastructure projects generate profits for corporations and political elites, often with state support.
- Displacement of Adivasis: Local communities, especially indigenous Adivasis, are forcibly displaced from their ancestral lands, losing their livelihoods, cultural heritage, and social networks.
- Marginalization: Displaced populations frequently receive inadequate compensation and lack access to new opportunities, leading to cycles of poverty and social exclusion.

This dynamic exposes the asymmetrical nature of development, where the costs and benefits are unevenly distributed, and the rhetoric of progress masks underlying processes of exploitation and exclusion.

Challenging Technocratic Narratives

The political economy approach critiques technocratic and apolitical narratives that present development as a matter of technical expertise, efficiency, or inevitable modernization. Such narratives often ignore:

- Class Dynamics: The ways in which different social classes experience and influence development.
- State-Corporate Alliances: The collusion between government and business interests in shaping policy and resource allocation.
- Historical Structures: The legacies of colonialism, land tenure systems, and social hierarchies that persist in shaping contemporary development.

By exposing these dynamics, the political economy approach calls attention to the politics of development—the struggles over land, resources, and representation that determine whose voices are heard and whose interests are prioritized.

Towards Democratic and Equitable Development

Recognizing the limitations and injustices of current development models, the political economy perspective advocates for:

- Democratic Participation: Ensuring that affected communities, especially marginalized groups like Adivasis, have a meaningful role in decision-making processes.
- Equitable Distribution: Designing policies that prioritize the fair distribution of benefits and burdens, including adequate compensation, rehabilitation, and access to opportunities for the displaced.
- Structural Transformation: Addressing the root causes of dispossession and inequality by reforming institutions, land rights, and governance mechanisms.

The political economy approach reveals that development is not merely about economic growth or technological advancement, but about power, justice, and social relations. By interrogating who wins and who loses, and by advocating for democratic and equitable alternatives, this perspective offers a critical lens for reimagining development in Jharkhand and beyond.

Development is not a neutral or universally beneficial process. Its meaning and consequences vary depending on the frameworks used to understand it. Classical theories celebrate industrial growth; critical theories expose the inequalities embedded in the development process. The Capability Approach centers human freedom, while political economy reveals the power dynamics behind policy choices.

To understand and address development-induced displacement, especially in regions like Jharkhand, we must draw from these diverse perspectives. Only then can we move toward a model of development that is just, inclusive, and sustainable.

Development, far from being a neutral or universally beneficial process, is a complex and contested phenomenon whose meaning and impact are shaped by the theoretical frameworks through which it is understood. Classical theories of development, such as modernization theory, often celebrate industrial growth, technological progress, and integration into the global economy as markers of advancement. These perspectives tend to view large-scale projects and economic expansion as inherently positive, sometimes overlooking the social and environmental costs they impose.

In contrast, critical theories—including dependency and world-systems approaches—highlight the deep inequalities and structural imbalances embedded in the development process. They reveal how development can perpetuate cycles of exploitation, marginalization, and dispossession, particularly for peripheral regions and vulnerable communities. These perspectives challenge the assumption that development automatically leads to shared prosperity, instead exposing how benefits are often concentrated among elites while costs are borne by the marginalized.

The Capability Approach, as articulated by Amartya Sen, shifts the focus from material outputs to human well-being, emphasizing the expansion of substantive freedoms and individual agency. This framework insists that true development should be measured by people's ability to lead lives they value, rather than by economic indicators alone. It draws attention to the ways in which displacement and loss of agency can undermine the very goals of development.

Finally, the political economy perspective underscores the power dynamics and institutional interests that shape development policies and their outcomes. It interrogates who makes decisions, who benefits, and who is excluded, revealing that development is often a site of contestation between competing interests.

To understand and address development-induced displacement, especially in contexts like Jharkhand, it is essential to draw on these diverse perspectives. Only by integrating insights from classical, critical, capability, and political economy approaches can we fully grasp the multifaceted nature of development and its consequences. Such a holistic understanding is crucial for designing policies and interventions that are just, inclusive, and sustainable—ensuring that development truly serves the needs and aspirations of all, rather than a privileged few.

CHAPTER FOUR

Adivasi Communities and Structural Exclusion

Adivasi or tribal communities form an integral and vibrant component of India's social and cultural fabric. Spread across various regions of the country, these communities possess distinct languages, customs, and knowledge systems that reflect deep ecological, historical, and spiritual ties to their ancestral lands. Despite their rich heritage and constitutional recognition as Scheduled Tribes, they continue to remain among the most marginalized and vulnerable sections of Indian society. The persistence of poverty, lack of access to quality education and healthcare, high rates of displacement, and political underrepresentation underscore the deep-rooted structural inequalities they face.

The state of Jharkhand, carved out of Bihar in the year 2000, was envisioned as a political and administrative entity that would safeguard the rights, identity, and autonomy of its predominantly tribal population. The demand for a separate state had emerged from decades of Adivasi-led movements that sought self-determination, control over natural resources, and protection from exploitative development. However, more than two decades since its formation, Jharkhand continues to reflect a stark contradiction: while created in the name of tribal empowerment, it has witnessed the intensification of processes that systematically exclude Adivasi communities from the benefits of development and governance.

This chapter undertakes a critical examination of this paradox by tracing the historical, structural, and institutional roots of Adivasi exclusion in Jharkhand. It delves into the colonial and post-colonial trajectories that shaped land tenure systems, forest laws, and state policies, which have long dispossessed tribal communities of their land and resources. It also investigates how institutional mechanisms, despite constitutional safeguards like the Fifth Schedule and the Panchayats (Extension to Scheduled Areas) Act (PESA), have often failed to ensure genuine autonomy or participatory governance for tribal populations.

Moreover, the chapter explores how contemporary models of development—especially those centered on mining, industrial expansion, and large infrastructure projects—have disproportionately impacted Adivasi areas. Instead of ushering in inclusive growth, these initiatives have frequently resulted in large-scale displacement, environmental degradation, and the erosion of traditional livelihoods, with little to no rehabilitation or restitution. In this context, development has often functioned not as a tool of empowerment, but as an instrument of exclusion, reinforcing patterns of dispossession and marginalization.

By examining these intersecting layers of historical injustice, structural inequality, and policy failure, the chapter aims to offer a nuanced understanding of the Adivasi experience in Jharkhand. It argues for a reimagining of development and governance paradigms that are grounded in tribal perspectives, rights, and aspirations, rather than imposed through top-down, extractive frameworks.

1. Colonial Categorization and Cultural Marginalization

The categorization of certain communities as "tribes" was not a neutral or benign administrative practice but a deeply political act that reflected and reinforced colonial and Brahmanical worldviews. British colonial administrators institutionalized the term "tribe" to identify and classify those social groups that did not conform to the dominant norms of the caste-based social hierarchy prevalent in much of the Indian subcontinent. These communities—many of whom lived in forested or hilly regions and followed distinct socio-cultural and economic systems—were portrayed as primitive, animistic, and pre-modern. This colonial taxonomy later formed the basis for the constitutional recognition of these groups as "Scheduled Tribes" after India's independence.

However, the conceptual underpinnings of this categorization were deeply flawed and rooted in orientalist and racialized discourses. British officials and ethnographers, influenced by 19th-century European theories of civilization and evolution, framed tribal communities as "isolated" and "uncivilized," lacking in history, culture, and governance. These stereotypes were not only reductive but also dehumanizing, as they denied the complexity, dynamism, and historical agency of Adivasi societies. The trope of the "noble savage" or the "wild aboriginal" became a recurring motif in colonial writings, casting tribal communities as objects of curiosity, subjects of reform, or threats to state order—never as equal political actors.

These colonial representations were not developed in isolation. They borrowed heavily from pre-existing Brahmanical and Sanskritic narratives that had long portrayed forest-dwelling peoples as *dasyus*, *rakshasas*, or *asuras*—figures symbolizing chaos, danger, and moral deviance in classical Hindu mythology. Such depictions served to demarcate the "civilized" Aryavarta from the "uncivilized" peripheries and justified the social and political exclusion of these groups. The British, in adopting and adapting these frameworks, found ideological justification for their own project of governance and control. By casting tribal communities as inherently different and incapable of self-rule, the colonial state legitimized paternalistic policies of surveillance, regulation, and intervention.

Through instruments such as the *Scheduled Districts Act (1874)*, the *Criminal Tribes Act (1871)*, and various forest laws, the British systematically isolated tribal communities from the emerging colonial economy and polity. Simultaneously, through ethnographic documentation and censuses, they reified tribal identities into rigid, bounded categories, ignoring the fluid, overlapping, and hybrid social realities on the ground. This essentialization laid the groundwork for structural "othering," where Adivasis were not only administratively separated but also epistemically excluded from the imagined national mainstream.

The long-term consequences of these colonial constructions are still visible in postcolonial India. While the Constitution sought to protect tribal rights through provisions such as the Fifth Schedule and affirmative action policies, the underlying assumptions about tribal backwardness and cultural inferiority have continued to influence state policies and popular perceptions. Thus, colonial categorization did not merely define tribal identity in the past—it continues to shape the terms of their marginalization in the present.

2. Post-Independence Policy and Adverse Inclusion

In the post-independence period, the Indian state adopted a framework of constitutional protections, special welfare programs, and administrative arrangements aimed at addressing the historical marginalization of Adivasi or tribal communities. The inclusion of tribal rights in the Constitution—most notably through the Fifth and Sixth Schedules, the recognition of Scheduled Tribes, and the provision of reservations in education, employment, and legislatures—reflected an acknowledgment of the need for affirmative state intervention. Moreover, tribal-majority regions were designated as "Scheduled Areas" to allow for tailored governance mechanisms that would account for the unique socio-cultural contexts of these communities.

However, this model of integration was deeply contradictory. While promising protection and empowerment, it simultaneously subjected Adivasi communities to the mainstream development paradigm that privileged economic growth, industrialization, and infrastructural expansion over ecological balance and cultural preservation. This led to what scholars describe as "adverse inclusion"—a condition in which tribal populations were not entirely excluded from the development process, but rather included on deeply disadvantageous and exploitative terms.

One of the most glaring manifestations of this adverse inclusion has been the disproportionate burden of displacement borne by tribal communities. Large-scale development projects—such as dams, thermal power plants, open-cast mines, and highways—have overwhelmingly been situated in mineral-rich but ecologically sensitive Adivasi regions, particularly in states like Jharkhand, Chhattisgarh, Odisha, and Madhya Pradesh. According to various estimates, while Adivasis constitute around 8% of India's population, they account for over 40% of those displaced by development-induced displacement since independence. This displacement has not only led to the physical uprooting of communities from their ancestral lands but has also resulted in the loss of cultural heritage, community cohesion, and traditional livelihoods tied to the forest and land.

Although the state has enacted progressive legislation to address these challenges—most notably the Panchayats (Extension to Scheduled Areas) Act, 1996 (PESA) and the Scheduled Tribes and Other Traditional Forest Dwellers (Recognition of Forest Rights) Act, 2006 (FRA)—their implementation has remained inconsistent, uneven, and often superficial. PESA was intended to extend self-governance to tribal areas by empowering Gram Sabhas (village assemblies) to manage local resources and approve development plans. Similarly, FRA sought to correct historical injustices by recognizing the customary rights of forest-dwelling communities over land and forest resources.

However, in practice, these legislative safeguards have frequently been undermined by bureaucratic inertia, lack of political will, and the vested interests of state and corporate actors. Gram Sabhas have often been bypassed in decisions involving land acquisition and forest clearance, while forest rights claims are routinely delayed, denied, or diluted. In many instances, state governments have prioritized extractive economic activities—such as mining and industrial expansion—over community consent and environmental sustainability, leading to renewed cycles of dispossession and resistance.

Moreover, the very language of development has often framed Adivasi communities as impediments to national progress—people who must be relocated, "rehabilitated," and "mainstreamed" for the sake of modernization. This reinforces a deeply paternalistic and assimilationist logic that ignores the pluralities of tribal life-worlds and undermines their agency. As a result, even as tribal communities are formally included within the ambit of the Indian state and its development agenda, the terms of this inclusion remain fundamentally unequal, coercive, and extractive.

In sum, the post-independence trajectory of tribal policy in India is marked by a troubling duality: a discourse of empowerment coexists with practices of dispossession. The promise of inclusive development has, for many Adivasis, translated into a lived reality of disempowerment through inclusion—a paradox that continues to shape the socio-political landscape of tribal regions like Jharkhand.

3. Social Exclusion in Practice

While legal frameworks and policy discourses often speak of inclusion and affirmative action for Scheduled Tribes, the everyday realities of Adivasi communities across India—particularly in states like Jharkhand—reveal a pervasive and deeply entrenched pattern of social exclusion. This exclusion is not merely a matter of economic deprivation but a multidimensional phenomenon encompassing lack of access to basic services, systemic discrimination, erosion of cultural identity, and political invisibility.

One of the most visible forms of exclusion is in the limited access to healthcare, education, and employment. Tribal-dominated regions consistently rank lower on key human development indicators compared to national averages. Healthcare infrastructure in these areas is often inadequate or entirely absent, with chronic shortages of medical personnel, poor transport connectivity, and cultural insensitivity in service delivery. Traditional healing practices and indigenous health knowledge are frequently dismissed or sidelined by mainstream health systems, leading to both mistrust and neglect.

In the sphere of education, high dropout rates, poor-quality schools, and the lack of culturally relevant curricula continue to hinder Adivasi children's learning outcomes. Teaching in unfamiliar languages and the absence of tribal history or worldview in textbooks further alienate students from their heritage, reinforcing a cycle of disengagement and underachievement. Even when Adivasi individuals acquire education or migrate to urban areas in search of better opportunities, they often face discrimination and stigmatization in schools, workplaces, and public spaces, being stereotyped as backward, unintelligent, or uncivilized.

This cultural alienation is compounded by the systemic denial of Adivasi voices in decision-making processes. Despite the constitutional and legal provisions mandating community participation—such as the role of Gram Sabhas under PESA or community consent under the Forest Rights Act—tribal populations are frequently excluded from the planning and implementation of policies that directly affect their lands, livelihoods, and futures. Local governance bodies are often co-opted by non-tribal elites, and state-led initiatives are rarely responsive to tribal needs or knowledge systems. The result is a form of governance that speaks in the language of inclusion but operates through mechanisms of marginalization.

Within this broader context, Adivasi women and youth experience layered and intersectional forms of exclusion. Women, in particular, bear the brunt of development-induced displacement and the breakdown of traditional economies. Their central role in subsistence agriculture, forest gathering, and household management is often rendered invisible in formal economic metrics. When displaced, Adivasi women not only lose access to economic resources but also suffer a decline in social status and decision-making power, as patriarchal norms become more entrenched in resettlement contexts.

Moreover, the dislocation of communities disrupts the transmission of cultural knowledge, oral traditions, and indigenous languages—key elements of Adivasi identity that are typically passed down through generations. For tribal youth, growing up in unfamiliar or hostile environments—urban slums, displacement camps, or assimilationist educational institutions—creates a sense of cultural disorientation and identity crisis. Many face the difficult challenge of navigating between the expectations of modern society and the heritage of their ancestors, often without the institutional or familial support to do so meaningfully.

Social exclusion, therefore, is not simply the absence of inclusion—it is the presence of structured inequality, cultural devaluation, and institutional neglect. In the case of Jharkhand and other tribal regions, this exclusion is both a legacy of historical injustices and a consequence of contemporary development and governance practices. Addressing it requires more than welfare interventions; it demands a radical rethinking of state-society relations, the valorization of indigenous knowledge, and the creation of participatory platforms that genuinely empower Adivasi communities, especially their women and youth.

4. Structural Inequality and Land Alienation

For Adivasi communities, land is not merely a source of livelihood but the foundation of social, cultural, and spiritual life. It is central to their identity, cosmology, and collective memory. Forests, rivers, hills, and fields are not just physical spaces but sacred landscapes imbued with ancestral significance, rituals, and traditional governance systems. The alienation of tribal land—whether through formal state acquisition, informal encroachment, or market-driven dispossession—represents not only economic displacement but also a profound rupture in the cultural and existential fabric of Adivasi society.

Despite the formal presence of constitutional and legal safeguards—most notably the Fifth Schedule of the Constitution, which provides for the protection of tribal interests in Scheduled Areas—Adivasis across India, and particularly in Jharkhand, continue to face widespread land dispossession. Several state-level laws, such as the Chotanagpur Tenancy (CNT) Act, 1908 and the Santhal Parganas Tenancy (SPT) Act, 1949, were historically enacted to restrict the transfer of tribal land to non-tribals. However, these protections have often been undermined by legal loopholes, poor enforcement, bureaucratic apathy, and collusion between local elites, corporations, and state authorities.

One major pathway of alienation has been the acquisition of land for public purpose projects—such as mining, dams, and industrial zones—under the guise of national development. The state has often invoked the doctrine of eminent domain to compulsorily acquire tribal lands, offering meager compensation and inadequate rehabilitation in return. In many cases, Adivasis are not even recognized as legal landholders, due to the lack of formal documentation, despite generations of customary possession. The Land Acquisition Acts, both colonial and post-colonial, have historically tilted in favor of the state and private capital, with little regard for the social costs borne by indigenous communities.

Further, illegal land transfers and encroachments—whether through manipulation of land records, fraudulent documentation, or political pressure—have become increasingly common, particularly as land values have risen in mineral-rich tribal areas. These processes often occur under the radar of formal law, facilitated by systemic corruption and the marginalization of tribal voices in administrative forums. Even when judicial remedies are sought, delays and procedural complexities mean that justice remains elusive for most Adivasi claimants.

This structural inequality in land ownership and access is not just a symptom of broader underdevelopment; it is a primary cause. Land alienation leads to loss of livelihoods, food insecurity, and forced migration, pushing many Adivasis into precarious urban informal sectors where they are further marginalized. Without land, tribal communities lose not only their economic base but also their autonomy, governance systems, and the intergenerational knowledge that is tied to specific ecological settings.

Moreover, the commodification of land as a market asset directly conflicts with the Adivasi worldview, which sees land as a shared, sacred resource to be collectively cared for rather than individually owned or traded. The intrusion of capitalist property relations into tribal areas has disrupted traditional forms of community ownership, leading to internal divisions, the erosion of customary institutions, and growing socio-economic stratification within tribal society itself.

In Jharkhand, where nearly 26% of the population is tribal, these processes have had especially severe consequences. Successive governments—despite electoral promises and symbolic gestures—have failed to protect tribal land rights in practice. Attempts to dilute tenancy laws, such as the proposed amendments to the CNT and SPT Acts in 2016, were met with widespread protests and eventually withdrawn. These moments of resistance underscore the centrality of land to tribal struggles and the deep mistrust Adivasis hold toward state institutions that are seen as complicit in their dispossession.

In sum, land alienation is not an accidental by-product of development but a structural feature of the socio-economic order that continues to marginalize Adivasi communities. It reflects deeper asymmetries of power, knowledge, and representation that deny tribal peoples the right to determine the use and meaning of their ancestral lands. Addressing this injustice requires not only legal reform and better enforcement but a fundamental shift in the state's approach—from one of control and extraction to one of partnership and respect for indigenous sovereignty.

5. Visualizing Exclusion: A Brief Timeline

- 1831–32: Kol Uprising against British land encroachment
- 1855–56: Santhal Rebellion in Jharkhand against landlords and British officials
- 1949: Integration of tribal regions into Indian state apparatus
- 1980s–1990s: Surge in mining, industrialization, and resistance movements in Jharkhand
- 2000: Formation of Jharkhand state with hopes of tribal empowerment
- 2006 onwards: Implementation of FRA and PESA, with mixed results

6. Mapping Marginalization

Jharkhand districts categorized by Scheduled Areas and Displacement Zones

Districts with Both Scheduled Area Status and Major Displacement:
Ranchi, Khunti, Lohardaga, Gumla, Simdega, Latehar, West Singhbhum, and East Singhbhum are districts that are both notified as Scheduled Areas and have witnessed significant displacement of Adivasi communities due to development projects.

Districts with Only Scheduled Area Status:
Saraikela Kharsawan, Dumka, Jamtara, Sahebganj, and Pakur are recognized as Scheduled Areas but have not been major displacement zones in recent years.

Districts with Major Displacement but Not Scheduled Areas:
Palamu and Garhwa, while not notified as Scheduled Areas, have experienced notable displacement due to industrial and mining activities.

Other Districts:
Godda and several others do not fall into either category prominently.

This spatial distribution underscores how the very regions meant to protect Adivasi rights are also the most affected by displacement, reflecting the paradox of development and marginalization in Jharkhand.

This bar chart visually categorizes Jharkhand districts by their status as Scheduled Areas, displacement zones, or both, making clear the overlap and distinctions among districts most affected by both protective legislation and development-induced displacement.

The marginalization of Adivasi communities in India—and particularly in Jharkhand—is not only social or economic, but also deeply spatial. A geographic analysis of development patterns, resource allocation, and displacement incidents reveals a stark and disturbing pattern: areas with the richest mineral deposits and most valuable natural resources consistently overlap with regions inhabited by tribal populations. This spatial coincidence is not accidental; rather, it underscores a systematic and structural process of targeting Adivasi territories for extractive and exploitative development.

Jharkhand, carved out in 2000 ostensibly to safeguard the rights, identity, and autonomy of its tribal population, is a striking case in point. The state holds over 40% of India's mineral wealth, including coal, iron ore, bauxite, uranium, and mica, yet remains one of the poorest and most underdeveloped in terms of human development indicators. A majority of these mineral-rich zones—such as in Singhbhum, Hazaribagh, Latehar, Godda, and Dumka—are simultaneously Scheduled Areas, demarcated for the protection of tribal communities under the Fifth Schedule of the Constitution. The juxtaposition of resource abundance and human deprivation reveals a deep contradiction at the heart of India's development model.

Using spatial mapping tools and Geographic Information Systems (GIS), researchers have consistently shown that zones of high mineral exploitation correspond closely with zones of high tribal displacement. For instance, open-cast mining and industrial corridors often cut through dense Adivasi Forest regions, displacing thousands of families, destroying sacred groves, and severing communities from their ecological lifeworlds. Infrastructure projects—such as highways, railways, power plants, and Special Economic Zones—have followed a similar pattern, carving up Adivasi land in the name of national interest while excluding them from its benefits.

This cartography of exclusion is compounded by state planning mechanisms that treat tribal land as a passive space for economic extraction rather than a lived and inhabited landscape with its own social, cultural, and ecological significance. Land acquisition plans, industrial policies, and investment zones are drawn up in capital cities and corporate boardrooms, with little or no participation from the communities they directly affect. In many cases, even Gram Sabhas are bypassed, despite constitutional and legal provisions mandating their consent under the Panchayats (Extension to Scheduled Areas) Act, 1996 (PESA).

Moreover, spatial marginalization is often internalized in urban planning and development schemes. Adivasi communities displaced by mega-projects and forced into urban peripheries or resettlement colonies are frequently ghettoized into informal settlements with inadequate housing, sanitation, and public services. They are rendered invisible in official maps and censuses, further compounding their political and social exclusion.

Importantly, mapping marginalization also reveals resistance. Across Jharkhand and other Adivasi regions, communities have used spatial tools and indigenous knowledge to demarcate community lands, map sacred sites, and assert traditional territorial rights. Participatory mapping initiatives have been employed as strategies to resist displacement, reclaim forest rights under the FRA, and document customary land use. These bottom-up cartographies challenge the dominant narratives of development and resource use, offering alternative visions grounded in sustainability, cultural continuity, and self-determination.

In essence, the spatial distribution of marginalization in India is not random but structurally produced. The overlap between tribal territories and resource frontiers reveals a deliberate development logic that views Adivasi land as an expendable commodity, ripe for extraction but dispensable in terms of social investment and political representation. Recognizing this spatial dynamic is crucial for any serious engagement with tribal justice, ecological democracy, and equitable development planning.

Conclusion

The structural exclusion of Adivasi communities in Jharkhand is not incidental or the result of isolated policy failures—it is the outcome of long-standing historical, social, and political processes that have deliberately marginalized tribal populations over time. From colonial classification and spatial segregation to post-independence development strategies that privilege capital-intensive growth over community-centered sustainability, the trajectory of state policy has consistently relegated Adivasi interests to the margins. This marginalization operates through a web of formal institutions and informal practices that together uphold systemic inequality, cultural erasure, and political invisibility.

Development, in its current form, is neither neutral nor universally beneficial. In Jharkhand, it has functioned less as a means of empowerment and more as a mechanism of dispossession. Resource extraction, infrastructure expansion, and industrialization—promoted under the banner of national interest—have disproportionately targeted Adivasi territories, leading to widespread land alienation, forced displacement, and the disruption of traditional livelihoods. The promise of modernity and progress often masks the violence of these processes, which uproot communities while offering little in terms of restitution, participation, or long-term benefit.

Crucially, this exclusion is not only economic but epistemic and political—Adivasi voices, knowledge systems, and worldviews are consistently excluded from the dominant frameworks that shape development policy. The state's reluctance to recognize collective rights, its failure to implement protective legislation like PESA and FRA effectively, and its preference for extractive partnerships with private capital all point to a deeper crisis of representation and justice.

This chapter has laid the groundwork for understanding the roots of tribal marginalization in Jharkhand by tracing the historical and institutional contours of exclusion. It has highlighted how state policies, legal frameworks, and socio-economic structures intersect to create conditions of "adverse inclusion"—where Adivasis are drawn into development processes on deeply unequal terms.

CHAPTER FIVE

Jharkhand's Political Economy and the Resource Curse

The Resource Curse and the Political Economy of Jharkhand

Jharkhand's status as one of India's most resource-rich yet economically underdeveloped states offers a textbook example of what scholars term the "resource curse" or the "paradox of plenty." Despite being endowed with immense mineral wealth—including nearly 40% of India's known reserves of coal, iron ore, bauxite, and uranium—the state remains beset by widespread poverty, low literacy rates, poor public health infrastructure, and stagnant human development indicators. This stark contrast between abundant natural wealth and chronic socio-economic deprivation raises fundamental questions about the model of development pursued in the region.

The explanation lies not in the mere presence of natural resources, but in the political economy that governs their extraction, distribution, and use. In Jharkhand, mining and related industrial activities have historically operated within a framework that disproportionately benefits external actors—state-owned enterprises, private corporations, and national elites—while local communities, especially Adivasis, bear the environmental, social, and cultural costs. Revenues from resource extraction are often funneled into centralized coffers or corporate profits, with minimal reinvestment in the regions from which they are derived.

This pattern of development reflects a deeper structural asymmetry, wherein Adivasi lands are treated as resource frontiers, valuable for their subsoil wealth but disregarded as social and cultural landscapes inhabited by politically marginalized communities. The state's developmental strategy, rooted in extractivism, has privileged capital-intensive, export-oriented industries over local, community-based modes of production. The focus has been on GDP growth, industrial output, and foreign investment—metrics that obscure the dispossession, displacement, and ecological degradation experienced by those on the ground.

The institutional architecture of Jharkhand has also played a role in perpetuating this paradox. Despite constitutional provisions and protective legislation aimed at safeguarding tribal rights—such as the Fifth Schedule, PESA, and the Forest Rights Act—implementation remains weak, inconsistent, and often deliberately obstructed. Administrative machinery in mineral-rich districts is frequently aligned more with corporate interests than with community welfare, creating a climate of mistrust, disenfranchisement, and resistance. Regulatory mechanisms meant to ensure environmental and social safeguards are regularly bypassed or diluted, and public hearings under environmental clearance processes are often reduced to formalities.

Moreover, corruption, elite capture, and weak governance have further distorted the potential benefits of mineral wealth. Successive state governments have been plagued by allegations of cronyism and collusion with mining interests, with little transparency or accountability in the allocation of mining leases and distribution of royalties. The result is a system where resource extraction serves the interests of a few, while the majority—especially tribal communities—experience increasing marginalization.

This condition is compounded by the lack of meaningful economic diversification. The overwhelming focus on mining has stunted the development of agriculture, education, and service sectors, leaving the local population with few alternatives for sustainable livelihoods. What employment mining does generate is often insecure, low-paid, and hazardous, with limited opportunities for skill development or upward mobility. At the same time, environmental degradation—deforestation, water pollution, and loss of biodiversity—has rendered traditional subsistence practices increasingly unviable.

Thus, the "resource curse" in Jharkhand is not simply a developmental anomaly but the consequence of deliberate policy choices and embedded structural inequalities. It reflects a model of growth that privileges short-term extraction over long-term sustainability, external interests over local agency, and centralized planning over grassroots participation. Rectifying this paradox will require a fundamental rethinking of development—one that centers equity, ecological balance, and tribal self-determination rather than extractive accumulation.

1. Historical Legacy of Extraction

The roots of Jharkhand's extractive economy run deep into the colonial period, when British administrators first identified the mineral-rich Chota Nagpur Plateau as a critical node for resource extraction. From the mid-19th century onwards, the region became the site of systematic exploitation, with mining outposts, railway lines, and administrative infrastructure built primarily to serve the needs of the British Empire. Key minerals such as coal, iron ore, mica, and copper were extracted and transported to industrial centers, with little concern for the welfare of local populations or the ecological impact of such activities.

This colonial model of development was based on a logic of resource appropriation and revenue maximization. Adivasi communities, who had long maintained sustainable relationships with their forests and lands, were often displaced or coerced into wage labor under harsh and exploitative conditions. Resistance movements—such as the Santhal Rebellion (1855-56) and the Birsa Munda Ulgulan (1899-1900)—emerged in direct response to this dispossession and the imposition of alien land and forest laws. However, the British response to such uprisings was militarized repression, coupled with the institutionalization of control over land, forests, and labor.

The colonial legacy of extractivism did not end with independence. Instead, it was repurposed and expanded by the Indian state under the guise of nation-building and economic modernization. Nationalized public sector undertakings (PSUs) such as Coal India, Steel Authority of India (SAIL), and Hindustan Copper Limited became the new agents of extraction. While the rhetoric of socialism and industrial development dominated the post-colonial discourse, the underlying model remained top-down, centralized, and extractive, often indifferent to the consent and rights of local populations.

The establishment of major industrial complexes such as Bokaro Steel Plant, Heavy Engineering Corporation in Ranchi, and uranium mines in Jaduguda exemplifies this continuity. These projects, though strategically important for India's economic ambitions, were frequently accompanied by large-scale displacement of Adivasi communities, loss of livelihoods, and environmental degradation. Compensation and rehabilitation were either inadequate or absent, and local participation in planning or governance was minimal.

Moreover, the creation of Jharkhand as a separate state in 2000, driven largely by Adivasi demands for autonomy and recognition, did little to disrupt this entrenched model. Instead, successive state governments have continued to court private investment in mining, power, and infrastructure, often under pressure from neoliberal economic policies and global capital. Land acquisition laws were diluted, forest clearances expedited, and environmental regulations weakened to facilitate large-scale industrial projects, many of which have replicated the colonial logic of extraction without redistribution.

This historical continuity of extractive development has not only impoverished local communities but has also locked Jharkhand into a resource-dependent economy vulnerable to market fluctuations, environmental crises, and political instability. It has undermined the possibility of alternative development paths rooted in community participation, ecological sustainability, and cultural preservation.

In sum, the historical legacy of extraction in Jharkhand is not a relic of the past but an ongoing structure that shapes contemporary patterns of inequality and resistance. Understanding this legacy is essential for deconstructing the narratives of progress that continue to justify dispossession and for envisioning a more equitable and inclusive future for the state's indigenous populations.

2. Industrial Projects and Displacement

Several large-scale industrial and mining projects have shaped the economic landscape of Jharkhand. Some of the most prominent include:

- **Bokaro Steel Plant (SAIL):** One of India's largest public sector undertakings, developed in the 1960s, which displaced thousands of local inhabitants.
- **Jamshedpur (Tata Steel):** A privately-led industrial township built in the early 20th century, long celebrated as a model of corporate-led

urbanisation, but with a legacy of displacing tribal communities.

- **Chandil Dam (Subarnarekha Project):** Intended for irrigation and hydroelectric purposes, this project led to displacement without adequate resettlement.
- **NTPC's North Karanpura Project:** A coal-based thermal power project that has raised environmental and displacement concerns in recent years.

In many cases, rehabilitation efforts have been poorly implemented or absent altogether. Local populations are rarely employed in these industries, further alienating them from the so-called development process.

3. Mining Policies and Governance Challenges

Jharkhand's abundant mineral wealth is embedded within a highly centralized policy framework, where decision-making power resides primarily with the central government and large corporate stakeholders, while local communities—especially Adivasis—are systematically excluded from meaningful participation. This centralized regime is codified in laws such as the Mines and Minerals (Development and Regulation) Act, 1957 (MMDR Act), which despite multiple amendments, continues to reflect a top-down approach to resource governance.

The 2015 amendment to the MMDR Act was heralded as a progressive step toward greater transparency and community benefit. It introduced the District Mineral Foundation (DMF) mechanism, which mandates that a portion of royalties from mining operations be allocated to local development in affected areas. Theoretically, DMFs are intended to fund infrastructure, health care, education, and livelihood programs for communities adversely impacted by mining activities.

However, in practice, the functioning of DMFs in Jharkhand has been plagued by systemic challenges. Studies and audit reports have repeatedly pointed to underutilization, diversion of funds, opaque accounting, and a lack of community involvement in project selection. Rather than empowering Gram Sabhas or local panchayats, the governance of DMFs is frequently concentrated in the hands of district bureaucrats and political elites, many of whom have limited accountability mechanisms. As a result, the DMF model has often reproduced the very developmental imbalances it was designed to mitigate.

Beyond inefficiencies in formal mechanisms, corruption and regulatory capture have emerged as persistent challenges in Jharkhand's mining sector.

There is ample evidence of collusion between state actors and private companies, resulting in the illegal allocation of leases, underreporting of extraction volumes, and manipulation of environmental clearances. The result is not only a substantial loss of public revenue but also accelerated environmental degradation—including deforestation, groundwater depletion, and air pollution—that disproportionately affects already vulnerable populations.

Illegal mining operations, often operating in connivance with local power brokers, are a particularly serious issue. These operations evade environmental norms, avoid tax and royalty obligations, and frequently operate without any form of social responsibility or redress for affected communities. The fragmented enforcement of mining laws and weak institutional capacity at the state level make it exceedingly difficult to monitor, regulate, or hold violators accountable.

Moreover, the centralized licensing process under the MMDR Act often ignores local consent, despite constitutional provisions such as PESA (1996) and the Forest Rights Act (2006), which require community approval for projects on tribal land. In many cases, mining leases are granted without prior informed consent from Gram Sabhas, violating both the spirit and the letter of these protective laws. This undermines not only tribal autonomy but also the legitimacy of state institutions in the eyes of the local population.

The governance deficits in Jharkhand's mining sector are thus multi-layered: they reflect legal ambiguities, institutional weaknesses, and deeper political-economic structures that privilege resource extraction over social justice. While the state continues to promote mining as a pathway to economic growth, the absence of transparent, accountable, and community-driven governance mechanisms has resulted in deepening socio-economic disparities, environmental destruction, and rising grassroots resistance.

If Jharkhand is to move beyond the extractive paradigm, there is an urgent need to reimagine mining governance—one that prioritizes local agency, ecological sustainability, and equitable benefit-sharing. Strengthening regulatory institutions, democratizing decision-making, and enforcing community rights are not merely administrative reforms—they are essential for reversing the historical trajectory of exclusion that has defined the state's mining economy.

4. Resource Curse in Action

The "resource curse" refers to the paradox where regions rich in natural resources experience slow economic growth, authoritarian governance, and social conflict. Jharkhand exemplifies this dynamic:

- **Economic Inequality:** Wealth generated from mining fails to trickle down. Adivasi communities remain landless and impoverished.
- **Political Instability:** Frequent government changes and weak institutional accountability hinder long-term development planning.
- **Conflict and Militarization:** Mineral zones often overlap with Maoist-affected areas, where local resistance is met with heavy policing.

5. Policy Implications and Alternatives

Despite the introduction of legal frameworks like PESA and the FRA, which are meant to empower local communities, implementation remains poor. A more just political economy would involve:

- Genuine consultation with affected communities.
- Transparent and accountable use of mining royalties.
- Investment in health, education, and local enterprise.
- Strengthening local governance institutions like Gram Sabhas.

Conclusion

Jharkhand's development trajectory starkly illustrates the deep and enduring contradictions between material resource abundance and human deprivation. Despite possessing a significant share of India's mineral wealth, the state remains mired in poverty, social inequality, and environmental degradation. This paradox—often termed the "resource curse"—is not merely an economic anomaly but a structural outcome of policies and governance frameworks that have historically prioritized extraction over equity, and profits over people.

The analysis presented in this chapter reveals that Jharkhand's underdevelopment is not a consequence of resource scarcity or lack of state intervention, but rather the result of systematic marginalization of Adivasi communities through historical, institutional, and political processes. From colonial-era dispossession to post-independence development models, tribal areas have been treated as resource frontiers—exploited for their mineral wealth without meaningful reinvestment in local well-being or recognition of indigenous rights. Governance mechanisms, including legislation such as the MMDR Act and the operation of District Mineral Foundations, have frequently failed to deliver justice or inclusion, owing to corruption, bureaucratic inertia, and elite capture.

Moreover, the displacement, cultural dislocation, and ecological devastation that accompany extractive development have disproportionately affected tribal populations, exacerbating their socio-economic vulnerabilities and weakening traditional knowledge systems. The promise of constitutional safeguards—such as the Fifth Schedule, PESA, and the Forest Rights Act—remains largely unfulfilled due to poor implementation and political resistance from vested interests.

Addressing this entrenched resource injustice requires more than policy tweaks or temporary welfare schemes. It demands a paradigm shift in the way development is conceptualized and practiced in Jharkhand. This shift must involve a move away from a centralized, top-down, extractive model toward a community-centered, participatory framework of governance. Such a model would place local voices at the heart of decision-making, recognize the intrinsic value of indigenous knowledge and land relations, and ensure that the benefits of natural wealth are equitably shared.

True development must be rooted in social justice, ecological sustainability, and democratic accountability. Jharkhand's future lies not in the blind pursuit of industrial growth, but in reimagining a developmental pathway where tribal autonomy, dignity, and rights are not secondary concerns but foundational principles. Only then can the state begin to reverse the cycles of exclusion and displacement that have characterized its history, and chart a more inclusive, equitable, and sustainable course forward.

CHAPTER SIX

UNDERSTANDING DEVELOPMENT-INDUCED DISPLACEMENT

Development-Induced Displacement (DID) refers to the involuntary relocation of individuals and communities from their ancestral lands and habitats as a direct consequence of large-scale development projects—such as dams, mining operations, highways, industrial zones, and urban expansion initiatives. Unlike displacement caused by natural disasters or conflict, DID is state-sanctioned and often justified under the rubric of "national interest," "economic growth," or "public purpose." However, in practice, such projects frequently result in severe disruptions to the lives, livelihoods, and cultural fabrics of affected communities.

In Jharkhand, a state marked by its rich endowment of natural resources and a high proportion of tribal population, development-induced displacement has become an enduring and systemic phenomenon. Since the colonial era—and more acutely after Independence—Adivasi communities have borne the brunt of displacement caused by coal mining, steel plants, uranium extraction, power projects, and infrastructure development. These processes have continued, and in many cases intensified, in the neoliberal era, with the state aggressively promoting investment in extractive and industrial sectors. The result is a recurring cycle of dispossession, in which the same communities are displaced multiple times over generations, often without adequate rehabilitation or compensation.

Crucially, DID in Jharkhand is not merely a logistical or administrative challenge—it is a deeply political and contested process. Land, in Adivasi worldviews, is not merely a commodity but a source of identity, spirituality, and collective memory. Forced displacement severs these intimate connections, leading to economic impoverishment, social disintegration, psychological trauma, and cultural loss. Moreover, compensation packages, when offered, are typically monetized and short-term, failing to restore the complex web of sustenance that tribal life is built upon. Legal safeguards meant to protect tribal land rights—such as the Fifth Schedule of the Constitution, PESA (1996), and the Forest Rights Act (2006)—are often bypassed or weakly enforced in the face of corporate and bureaucratic interests.

This chapter seeks to unpack the multidimensional nature of development-induced displacement in Jharkhand. It explores the mechanisms through which displacement is legitimized and executed, examines the socio-economic and cultural consequences for displaced communities, and highlights the ways in which resistance is articulated through protests, legal battles, and grassroots mobilization. By doing so, the chapter aims to situate DID not as an inevitable byproduct of progress, but as a contested terrain where competing visions of development, justice, and identity collide.

1. Forms and Causes of Displacement

DID in Jharkhand stems from a range of development initiatives:

- Mining: Coal, iron ore, and bauxite mining has led to the eviction of communities, destruction of forests, and pollution of land and water.
- Dams and Hydroelectric Projects: Projects like the Subarnarekha Dam have submerged villages and uprooted thousands.
- Industrial Townships and SEZs: Private and public sector undertakings such as Bokaro Steel Plant and industrial corridors have displaced local populations with minimal consultation.
- Urban Expansion: Cities like Ranchi and Jamshedpur have grown by absorbing peri-urban tribal settlements, often without formal rehabilitation.

2. Legal and Institutional Frameworks

Several laws govern land acquisition and resettlement, including:

- Land Acquisition Act (1894; replaced by the LARR Act 2013): Historically used for acquiring land with limited provisions for rehabilitation.

- PESA (1996): Grants decision-making powers to Gram Sabhas in Scheduled Areas but is poorly enforced.
- FRA (2006): Recognizes individual and community forest rights but faces bureaucratic hurdles.

Despite these legal safeguards, implementation remains weak. Displacement often occurs through bureaucratic fiat or manipulated consent processes.

3. Consequences of Displacement

- Economic: Loss of agricultural land and forests leads to unemployment, food insecurity, and increased dependence on wage labor.
- Social: Displacement fractures kinship networks, disrupts community institutions, and erodes traditional support systems.
- Cultural: Sacred groves, burial grounds, and heritage sites are often destroyed, leading to cultural alienation.
- Psychological: Feelings of betrayal, trauma, and helplessness are common among displaced persons.

4. Gendered Dimensions of Displacement

The experience of displacement is profoundly gendered, with Adivasi women bearing the brunt of its adverse impacts in unique and often overlooked ways. While development-induced displacement disrupts entire communities, it imposes disproportionate burdens on women, compounding existing inequalities of power, access, and recognition. Understanding the gendered dimensions of displacement is essential to developing just and inclusive policy responses.

Loss of Economic Autonomy

In many Adivasi societies, women have traditionally played a central role in subsistence agriculture, forest gathering, livestock care, and local exchange economies. Their access to and control over common resources—such as land, water, and forest produce—not only sustains households but also gives them a measure of economic autonomy and social status. Displacement severs these ties to land and ecology, rendering women economically dependent on male family members, government schemes, or exploitative informal labor markets. Compensation, when provided, is typically registered in the name of male heads of households, reinforcing patriarchal ownership patterns and sidelining women's economic rights.

Heightened Vulnerability to Violence and Exploitation

The upheaval caused by displacement often results in increased domestic burdens, emotional stress, and social insecurity, particularly in unfamiliar resettlement environments. The loss of community networks, privacy, and support systems heightens women's exposure to domestic violence, sexual harassment, and trafficking. Displaced women, especially young girls and widows, are at greater risk of forced labor, early marriage, or being pushed into exploitative urban economies. In resettlement colonies, where basic infrastructure is often inadequate, women face daily struggles for water, sanitation, and safety—issues that remain invisible in formal rehabilitation plans.

Exclusion from Decision-Making and Representation

Despite being deeply affected by displacement, women's voices are routinely excluded from key processes of consultation, negotiation, and planning. Meetings with government officials and project authorities are often male-dominated, with women either absent or silenced by social norms. Even in structures meant to ensure representation—such as Gram Sabhas under the Panchayat (Extension to Scheduled Areas) Act (PESA)—women's participation is frequently tokenistic. The lack of gender-sensitive policy frameworks means that women's specific concerns—such as loss of childcare networks, reproductive health, or culturally significant spaces—are rarely acknowledged, let alone addressed.

Disruption of Cultural and Social Roles

Displacement also leads to the disintegration of traditional cultural roles held by women in Adivasi societies. Rituals, festivals, healing practices, and oral traditions that were centered around the land and natural cycles are often disrupted or lost altogether. With the erosion of these roles, women experience not just material loss but also symbolic and psychological marginalization. The dislocation from land is thus not only a physical rupture but also a spiritual and intergenerational break, where women struggle to pass on cultural knowledge to younger generations in unfamiliar and often hostile settings.

In sum, the gendered dimensions of development-induced displacement are multifaceted and severe. Adivasi women face invisible yet profound forms of dispossession that go beyond the economic to touch upon bodily autonomy, identity, safety, and voice. Any policy or developmental intervention that fails to account for these dimensions risks deepening gender inequalities and reproducing cycles of marginalization.

Moving forward, there is an urgent need for gender-sensitive displacement and rehabilitation policies that ensure women's meaningful participation, access to compensation, protection from violence, and support for rebuilding livelihoods and social networks. Recognizing women not as passive victims but as agents of resistance, knowledge-keepers, and leaders is key to imagining more just and inclusive forms of development in Jharkhand and beyond.

5. Case Snapshots from Jharkhand

- Koel-Karo Project: A proposed hydroelectric dam which was stalled after mass protests by tribal villagers who feared loss of sacred sites and agricultural land.
- North Karanpura Coalfields: Thousands displaced for NTPC's coal extraction project. Rehabilitation packages remain pending, and many have turned to precarious informal labor.
- Netarhat Field Firing Range: Originally planned for military training, the project faced tribal opposition due to land acquisition without consent, reflecting militarized displacement.

6. Resistance and Contestation

Displacement in Jharkhand is not a one-sided narrative of victimhood—it is also a history of resilience, resistance, and collective assertion. Adivasi communities have not passively accepted the erosion of their rights, identity, and livelihoods. Instead, they have emerged as active political agents, mounting sustained struggles against displacement and extractive development through a combination of grassroots mobilization, legal intervention, and alliance-building.

At the heart of this resistance lies the powerful slogan "Jal, Jangal, Zameen" (Water, Forest, Land)—a rallying cry that encapsulates the Adivasi worldview, in which land is not a mere economic resource but the basis of life, spirituality, and cultural identity. This triad symbolizes a holistic relationship with nature that stands in stark contrast to the state's commodified, profit-driven conception of development. It also reflects a vision of justice rooted in autonomy, sustainability, and collective rights.

Historically, Jharkhand has witnessed numerous grassroots uprisings against forced displacement—from the Koel-Karo anti-dam movement, which successfully stalled a large hydropower project in the 1980s and

1990s, to the Pathalgadi movement in recent years, which invoked constitutional provisions to assert local self-rule under the Fifth Schedule and PESA. These struggles are not merely about resisting specific projects but are part of a broader claim to dignity, self-determination, and democratic participation.

Resistance has taken multiple forms:

- Mass protests, rallies, and sit-ins (dharna) at project sites and government offices.
- Legal advocacy through Public Interest Litigations (PILs) and interventions in courts to uphold constitutional rights and land protections.
- Social audits and fact-finding missions that document rights violations, often in collaboration with civil society organizations and journalists.
- Media engagement, both traditional and digital, to publicize displacement narratives and challenge official narratives.
- Solidarity networks with national and international human rights groups, academic institutions, and indigenous movements, amplifying the cause of displaced communities beyond local geographies.

Despite the strength of these movements, state responses have often been coercive and repressive. Protestors are frequently branded as "anti-development" or even "anti-national," and subjected to intimidation, surveillance, arbitrary arrests, and police violence. Activists and community leaders have been charged under sedition laws or the Unlawful Activities (Prevention) Act (UAPA), stifling democratic dissent. Such repression reflects a larger trend of shrinking civic space and the criminalization of resistance in the name of national interest and investment promotion.

Yet, in the face of adversity, Adivasi resistance in Jharkhand continues to endure and evolve. It is rooted in deep historical memory, drawing inspiration from earlier movements for land rights and tribal autonomy—from the Santhal Hul (1855) and Birsa Munda's Ulgulan (1899–1900) to the Jharkhand statehood movement itself. These legacies inform contemporary struggles and remind us that the demand for "development with dignity" is not a recent invention but a longstanding quest.

In essence, the contestation over development-induced displacement is not just about compensation or rehabilitation—it is about who has the right to define development, who benefits from it, and whose voices matter in shaping the future. As this chapter demonstrates, resistance in Jharkhand is a vibrant assertion of tribal sovereignty, environmental justice, and alternative imaginations of progress that challenge the dominant extractive paradigm.

Conclusion

Development-induced displacement in Jharkhand exposes a deep and enduring crisis of justice, democracy, and accountability. Far from being an unfortunate but necessary byproduct of national progress, displacement in this context is a structural injustice—one that disproportionately burdens Adivasi communities while privileging external corporate interests and state agendas. Though framed in public discourse as a pathway to modernization, industrial growth, and national development, the actual costs of development are borne by those least responsible for shaping its course and least likely to benefit from its outcomes.

For displaced communities, particularly Adivasis, displacement is not merely a relocation from one place to another—it is a rupture of identity, culture, economy, and dignity. It erodes their symbiotic relationship with land and forests, fragments their social networks, and pushes them to the margins of urban and rural life where they often face exclusion, precarity, and invisibility. In this light, displacement is not simply a logistical problem to be solved through compensation and resettlement packages; it is a moral and political crisis that demands urgent rethinking of both the means and ends of development.

Despite constitutional guarantees and legislative protections—such as the Fifth Schedule, PESA, and the Forest Rights Act—there exists a persistent gap between law and practice, rights and realities. State agencies and private actors often bypass or undermine these frameworks through opaque decision-making, weak implementation, and coercive tactics. As a result, communities are not just displaced physically but also excluded institutionally—from governance, legal redress, and developmental planning.

To move forward, a fundamental paradigm shift is necessary. Displacement must be approached not as an administrative necessity or technical challenge but as a question of human rights, democratic participation, and ethical governance. This means ensuring that affected communities are active participants, not passive recipients, in decisions that impact their land, lives, and futures. It also requires transparent processes, fair compensation, holistic rehabilitation, and above all, a commitment to protecting cultural and ecological integrity.

Ultimately, the story of development-induced displacement in Jharkhand is not just about what has been lost, but also about what could still be reclaimed—justice, dignity, and the right to a future on one's own terms.

CHAPTER SEVEN

FIELD REALITIES: VOICES FROM DISPLACED COMMUNITIES

While statistics, official reports, and policy documents offer important insights into the scope and scale of development-induced displacement, they often fail to capture the emotional, cultural, and human dimensions of what it truly means to be displaced. Numbers can quantify how many people have lost their homes or how much land has been acquired—but they cannot convey the grief of losing ancestral land, the silence of disrupted rituals, or the trauma of being rendered invisible in one's own homeland.

This chapter seeks to bridge that gap between abstract data and lived reality by presenting a series of first-hand narratives and oral histories from Adivasi individuals and families displaced by different development projects across Jharkhand. These include mega-dams, coal mining operations, industrial corridors, and urban expansion plans. Taken together, these stories paint a vivid and often heart-wrenching picture of dispossession, dislocation, and struggle.

The narratives reveal a shared pattern of experience:

- Loss of land, livelihood, and cultural belonging.
- Resistance against forced acquisition and bureaucratic coercion.
- Adaptation to new and often hostile environments.

- And, perhaps most powerfully, a remarkable resilience in the face of systemic injustice.

Many of those displaced speak of broken promises—of compensation that never arrived, of rehabilitation sites that lacked basic amenities, and of being told their sacrifice was for the nation, even as they were left behind in its progress. Others reflect on the emotional cost of displacement: the pain of leaving behind sacred groves, community burial grounds, or the trees their ancestors planted. Women speak of the violence of silence—of not being consulted, not being counted, and not being heard. Youth express the anguish of identity rupture, as they struggle to reconcile ancestral ways of life with the pressures of urban poverty.

Yet, these narratives are not only stories of loss. They are also stories of resistance and survival—of people organizing protests, reclaiming rights through the courts, rebuilding livelihoods, and reviving cultural traditions. In recounting these lived experiences, this chapter underscores the agency and dignity of displaced communities, refusing to reduce them to mere victims or statistics.

In doing so, it invites the reader to see displacement not just as a policy failure or an economic cost, but as a moral and human crisis that demands empathy, accountability, and transformative change. These voices challenge us to reimagine development from the margins, centering those who have borne its heaviest burdens without reaping its promised rewards.

1. Voices from the Subarnarekha Dam Project

The Subarnarekha Multipurpose Project submerged dozens of villages in East Singhbhum. When interviewed, an elderly woman named Kamli Devi recalled:

"They told us we would get new land and houses. But years passed, and we received nothing. My family now works as laborers in Jamshedpur. We were farmers. We had fields, cattle, and festivals. Now we live in a rented slum."

Despite promises of resettlement, many affected families were either left out of the official lists or received compensation inadequate for rebuilding their lives.

2. Displacement in the North Karanpura Region

Adivasi villagers in Chatra district described how their lands were acquired for the NTPC project without their informed consent. One resident, Birsa Munda (name changed), stated:

"We were not consulted. The officials came with papers and security. They told us the project is for the nation's progress. But what about us? Are we not part of the nation?"

Local protests were often met with arrests and police repression. Many families now live in transition camps, relying on irregular manual labor to survive.

3. The Silent Displacement of Women

Women rarely feature in compensation registers or land deeds. Yet their displacement is deeply personal:

"After the mining started, my days changed. I used to collect firewood and tend to my goats. Now the forest is gone, and my daughters cannot go to school safely," said Savitri, a mother of three in Latehar.

Women face not only loss of livelihoods but also threats to their dignity, safety, and autonomy.

4. Cultural Erosion and Spiritual Loss

For many tribal families, displacement also means the desecration of sacred groves, burial sites, and ancestral lands:

"Our sarna sthal was buried under coal ash. No amount of money can bring it back," shared a village elder from Hazaribagh.

Such spiritual dislocation is rarely accounted for in resettlement policies.

5. Stories of Resistance and Hope

In spite of these hardships, communities have demonstrated incredible resilience. Youth in Dumka district have organized themselves into advocacy groups demanding implementation of PESA. Women's collectives in Khunti have started income-generating cooperatives to regain economic control.

"We may not stop the companies, but we will not disappear quietly," declared Meena, an activist from a displaced community.

Conclusion

These stories offer a powerful and necessary counter-narrative to the sanitized, often celebratory tone of official accounts of development. Government documents, corporate reports, and mainstream discourse frequently frame large infrastructure and industrial projects as symbols of national progress, economic growth, and modernization. Yet the lived experiences of those displaced reveal a very different truth—one marked by disruption, dispossession, and a profound sense of erasure.

The voices of the displaced remind us that displacement is not merely about the loss of land—it is about the loss of life in all its fullness. It is about the severing of age-old relationships with soil, forests, rivers, and sacred spaces. It is about disrupted rhythms—seasonal cycles of cultivation, community festivals, oral storytelling traditions, and everyday routines that rooted people in place and gave meaning to time. It is about the fading of memories tied to ancestral homes, village landmarks, and collective rituals. It is about the weakening of relationships within communities, strained by forced relocation and the breakdown of trust in institutions that were supposed to protect them.

These narratives challenge the dominant development paradigm, urging us to rethink what development means and for whom it is intended. They expose the limitations of compensation packages, which may provide monetary relief but cannot restore a way of life. They highlight the inadequacy of resettlement schemes that focus on shelter and infrastructure while ignoring social cohesion, cultural continuity, and psychological healing. Most importantly, they underscore the silencing of marginalized voices in decision-making processes that profoundly affect their futures.

Listening to these voices—with sincerity, humility, and accountability—is not just an act of empathy; it is a political and ethical imperative. Their stories must inform how we design, implement, and evaluate development policies. Only by centering the lived realities of those at the receiving end of displacement can we begin to craft approaches that honor human dignity, protect collective rights, and prioritize social justice over abstract economic metrics.

In this sense, these stories do more than recount suffering—they offer insight, wisdom, and resistance. They compel us to imagine an alternative model of development—one that is participatory, inclusive, and rooted in the lived needs and aspirations of local communities. They urge us to move from a politics of extraction to a politics of care.

CHAPTER EIGHT

RESISTANCE, RESILIENCE, AND POLICY RESPONSES

Displacement is not only a process of loss and disempowerment; it is also a catalyst for political awakening and collective action. While development-induced displacement in Jharkhand has caused widespread suffering—uprooting people from their land, livelihoods, and cultural moorings—it has also ignited a powerful and sustained response from those affected. This chapter explores how displaced Adivasi communities have transformed their pain into protest, their marginalization into mobilization, and their exclusion into a demand for recognition, justice, and rights.

Far from being passive victims, many displaced individuals and groups have emerged as political actors, organizing themselves into grassroots movements, alliances, and legal campaigns. Their struggles have taken multiple forms: road blockades, mass rallies, hunger strikes, occupation of project sites, and formal petitions to courts and human rights commissions. Slogans like *"Jal, Jangal, Zameen"* (Water, Forest, Land) have become more than rallying cries—they embody a political philosophy rooted in indigenous values of stewardship, autonomy, and resistance to extractive models of development.

This chapter delves into key movements across the state—such as the Koel-Karo anti-dam agitation, the Netarhat anti-firing range protests, and the Pathalgadi movement—to illustrate how displacement has spurred the formation of new political subjectivities. These movements are not only reactive; they are proactive assertions of tribal self-determination and constitutional rights, often grounded in provisions like the Fifth Schedule, PESA, and the Forest Rights Act (FRA). In these contexts, the politics of displacement becomes inseparable from the politics of identity, land, and democratic participation.

Equally important is the examination of how the state has responded to such mobilizations. On one hand, state institutions have occasionally engaged with displaced communities through negotiated settlements, land restoration, or delayed project implementation. On the other hand, responses have also included repression, criminalization of dissent, use of police force, and the strategic deployment of development rhetoric to delegitimize resistance. Activists have been arrested, movements branded as anti-national, and communities divided through co-option and fear.

Alongside the state, civil society organizations, legal aid groups, journalists, and academic allies have played an important role in amplifying the voices of displaced communities. Their interventions—ranging from legal representation in courts and public interest litigation to media campaigns, human rights monitoring, and policy critiques—have helped keep the issue of displacement visible in public discourse. However, civil society's engagement remains uneven and sometimes urban-centric, highlighting the need for more sustained and grassroots-driven alliances.

In evaluating these dynamics, this chapter argues that displacement is not merely a humanitarian crisis—it is a site of political contestation and transformation. It forces a reckoning with the meaning of citizenship, justice, and democracy in a developmental state like India. The resilience and political consciousness of displaced communities in Jharkhand thus offer both a critique of mainstream development models and a blueprint for more equitable, accountable, and participatory alternatives.

1. The Rise of Local Movements

The experience of displacement in Jharkhand has given rise to robust and persistent grassroots movements, led by Adivasi communities determined to defend their rights, livelihoods, and cultural identity. These movements have not only resisted the immediate threats of eviction and land acquisition but have also forged long-term strategies of political assertion and legal empowerment. Far from being spontaneous or fragmented, these mobilizations are rooted in deep histories of indigenous resistance and have evolved into organized platforms for democratic participation and rights-based advocacy.

• Koel-Karo Jan Sangathan (KKJS)

Perhaps the most iconic of these movements, the Koel-Karo Jan Sangathan emerged in the 1970s to oppose the proposed Koel-Karo hydroelectric project, which threatened to submerge over 135 villages and displace tens of thousands of tribal families. The movement mobilized communities across the affected districts through non-violent protest marches, sit-ins (dharnas), and cultural festivals that celebrated tribal heritage and solidarity. Women played a central role in this resistance, often leading protests and forming the backbone of local coordination.

What made KKJS unique was its use of traditional institutions such as gram sabhas and its emphasis on cultural resistance—invoking ancestral connections to the land and forest spirits (*sarhul, jatra*) as part of their political claim. After decades of sustained opposition and a historic incident in 2001 where police firing killed several protestors, public support for the project dwindled. Ultimately, the Koel-Karo project was shelved, marking one of India's most significant people-led victories against large-scale displacement.

• Jharkhand Mines Area Coordination Committee (JMACC)

Another notable platform is the Jharkhand Mines Area Coordination Committee (JMACC), a coalition of community leaders, legal practitioners, environmentalists, and activists working across multiple mining-affected regions. JMACC plays a critical role in monitoring violations of environmental and land laws, challenging illegal land acquisition in courts, and pushing for the proper implementation of rehabilitation and resettlement (R&R) policies.

JMACC is especially active in regions like Hazaribagh, Latehar, and West Singhbhum, where mining operations by both public and private entities have led to massive displacement. It helps communities access legal remedies, build awareness of their constitutional rights, and track the use and misuse of District Mineral Foundation (DMF) funds meant for local development. Its efforts represent a strategic shift from reactive protest to institutional engagement and policy advocacy.

• Adivasi Mahasabhas and Gram Sabhas

At the local level, Adivasi Mahasabhas—collective forums of tribal elders, women, and youth—along with statutory gram sabhas (village assemblies) have increasingly invoked constitutional provisions such as the Panchayat (Extension to Scheduled Areas) Act (PESA), 1996, to assert control over their land and resources. PESA grants special powers to gram sabhas in Scheduled Areas, including the right to be consulted on land acquisition and the management of natural resources.

In villages across Simdega, Gumla, Khunti, and other tribal-majority districts, gram sabhas have passed resolutions rejecting land acquisition, conducted their own community mapping exercises, and organized local referenda to determine consent for development projects. These actions represent a significant assertion of grassroots democracy, rooted in indigenous values of consensus and collective decision-making.

Together, these local movements have redefined the landscape of resistance in Jharkhand. They highlight how displaced communities are not merely victims but agents of political transformation, challenging top-down development and asserting an alternative vision based on justice, autonomy, and ecological stewardship. Their struggles also serve as living reminders that true development cannot proceed without the meaningful participation and consent of those whose lives and lands are at stake.

2. Legal Interventions and Constitutional Protections

Tribal communities and allied organizations have used legal frameworks to challenge displacement:

- Public Interest Litigations (PILs): Filed in High Courts and the Supreme Court to contest land acquisition procedures, environmental clearances, and implementation gaps in rehabilitation policies.
- Use of PESA and FRA: Tribes have cited these acts to claim collective rights over forests and common lands. In some areas, Gram Sabhas have successfully blocked land transfers.
- Judicial Precedents: Court rulings have occasionally supported tribal rights, setting legal precedents for consent and consultation.

3. Role of Civil Society and NGOs

In the complex terrain of development-induced displacement in Jharkhand, civil society organizations and NGOs have emerged as indispensable allies of marginalized and displaced communities. Operating at the intersection of advocacy, service delivery, and capacity building, these organizations have helped amplify the voices of the affected, bridge the gap between state policies and grassroots realities, and contest the dominant narratives of development that often exclude or erase tribal perspectives.

One of the most critical roles civil society actors play is in offering legal and institutional support. Displaced communities often lack access to legal literacy, representation, and procedural knowledge. NGOs have stepped in to provide legal aid, draft petitions, represent communities in courts and quasi-judicial bodies, and ensure that constitutional provisions—such as the Fifth Schedule, PESA (1996), and the Forest Rights Act (2006)—are not just symbolic promises but enforceable rights. In many instances, they have helped halt illegal evictions, secure land titles, and demand accountability from government agencies.

Another important contribution is the facilitation of social audits and fact-finding missions. By documenting instances of forced displacement, environmental degradation, or violations of human rights, civil society organizations serve as watchdogs, producing credible evidence that counters official statistics or sanitized reports. These audits often bring to light discrepancies between claims of "rehabilitation" and the lived reality of people resettled in inhospitable and poorly serviced colonies. Through research reports, policy briefs, and media engagement, NGOs have kept the issue of displacement in the public and policy discourse.

Civil society actors also focus on mobilizing youth, women, and other marginalized segments within Adivasi communities, who are often sidelined even within resistance movements. They conduct leadership training, community media workshops, and education programs that empower these groups to articulate their experiences and advocate for their rights. In doing so, NGOs foster inclusive and intersectional activism, ensuring that resistance is not just reactive but also forward-looking and equitable.

Organizations like the Bindrai Institute for Research and Social Action (BIRSA) have been at the forefront of this work. BIRSA has documented land alienation, displacement patterns, and environmental degradation, while also helping communities file claims under the Forest Rights Act and challenge unlawful land transfers. Its research-oriented activism blends data with grassroots voices, offering a grounded critique of state-led development policies.

Similarly, the Jharkhand Indigenous People's Forum (JIPF) serves as a vital platform for articulating tribal worldviews and resisting homogenizing models of development. It organizes consultations, tribal conventions, and public hearings to create spaces where Adivasi epistemologies, values, and priorities are centered rather than marginalized. These forums have strengthened solidarity among tribal groups and built bridges with national and international human rights organizations.

In addition, partnerships between NGOs and academic institutions, media outlets, and international advocacy networks have globalized the struggle of Jharkhand's displaced communities. Such collaborations have helped raise awareness at UN forums, attract attention from global environmental watchdogs, and subject multinational corporations to transnational accountability frameworks.

Yet, it is important to recognize that civil society's impact is not uniform. Some NGOs have faced constraints due to regulatory crackdowns, funding limitations, or political pressures, especially under tightening frameworks like the Foreign Contribution Regulation Act (FCRA). Despite these challenges, many organizations have continued their work with courage and creativity, redefining development as a process grounded in justice, participation, and sustainability.

4. Policy Reforms and Their Limitations

In response to mounting resistance, the state has introduced policy reforms:

- LARR Act 2013: Emphasizes consent, social impact assessment, and fair compensation. Yet, loopholes and weak enforcement undermine its effectiveness.
- District Mineral Foundation (DMF): Aimed at using mining royalties for local development. However, funds are often misused or diverted.
- Rehabilitation Policies: While updated policies exist on paper, their execution remains inconsistent, often lacking transparency and accountability.

5. Emerging Strategies of Resistance and Resilience

- Community Media: Adivasi youth are increasingly using social media, photography, and film to document displacement and mobilize support.
- Ecological Resistance: Some villages have revived traditional ecological practices to assert their stewardship of natural resources.
- Transnational Solidarity: Alliances with international human rights organizations and global indigenous movements have added legitimacy and visibility to local struggles.

Conclusion

The story of development-induced displacement in Jharkhand is not solely one of dispossession—it is equally a testament to the resilience, agency, and political consciousness of its displaced communities. In the face of systemic exclusion, state repression, and broken promises of rehabilitation, Adivasi communities have not remained passive victims. Instead, they have drawn strength from their deep-rooted collective identity, ancestral memory, and cultural attachment to land, transforming trauma into resistance and marginalization into mobilization.

The resistance movements that have emerged—whether through grassroots protests, legal battles, or the assertion of traditional governance through gram sabhas—have gone beyond opposing displacement. They have redefined what development means, challenging dominant state and corporate narratives that equate progress with extraction, infrastructure, and GDP growth. For displaced Adivasis, development is not about highways and industrial corridors—it is about dignity, sovereignty over natural resources, sustainable livelihoods, and cultural continuity. In this sense, their movements are not only reactive but deeply visionary, offering alternative paradigms rooted in ecological balance, participatory democracy, and social justice.

At the same time, these struggles have exposed the limitations of India's institutional mechanisms in addressing the deep moral and political crisis at the heart of displacement. Legal rights and constitutional provisions have too often remained on paper. Nevertheless, civil society efforts, grassroots organizing, and solidarity across movements have managed to keep these rights alive in practice, even under difficult circumstances.

As we move forward, it is crucial to ask: Can India's existing legal and institutional frameworks rise to the challenge of ensuring justice for the displaced? Do international human rights norms, environmental covenants, and development ethics offer meaningful avenues for redress? Or do they, too, risk being co-opted by the very structures they seek to regulate?

CHAPTER NINE

GLOBAL NORMS AND INDIA'S INSTITUTIONAL FRAMEWORK

Introduction: Global Dimensions of Displacement

Displacement caused by development is not merely a localized or national phenomenon—it is a global crisis that sits at the intersection of economic growth, human rights, and environmental sustainability. Across the world, Indigenous and marginalized communities are being uprooted from their ancestral lands to make way for infrastructure projects, mining operations, special economic zones, and urban expansion. In response, the international community has evolved a complex web of norms, principles, and regulatory frameworks aimed at mitigating the adverse impacts of such displacement and upholding the rights of affected populations.

Key global institutions—such as the United Nations, the World Bank, the International Labour Organization (ILO), and various environmental treaty bodies—have formulated standards and conventions that recognize the special vulnerabilities of Indigenous peoples and stress the importance of free, prior, and informed consent (FPIC), participatory development, and just rehabilitation. For example, the United Nations Declaration on the Rights of Indigenous Peoples (UNDRIP) emphasizes the right of Indigenous communities to determine their own development pathways and to give or withhold consent for projects affecting their land, territories, and resources. Likewise, the World Bank's Environmental and Social Framework includes specific safeguards for involuntary resettlement and Indigenous peoples, requiring comprehensive impact assessments and inclusive consultation processes.

In the Indian context, these international frameworks are particularly relevant given the scale of development-induced displacement (DID) and the persistent gaps in domestic implementation of constitutional safeguards and statutory protections such as the Panchayats (Extension to Scheduled Areas) Act (PESA) and the Forest Rights Act (FRA). Jharkhand, with its mineral-rich landscape and high concentration of Scheduled Tribes, stands at the epicenter of these contradictions. Here, global norms are not abstract ideals—they have direct bearing on the lived experiences of displaced Adivasi communities, who are often caught between state-led development ambitions and the erosion of their cultural, economic, and ecological foundations.

This chapter critically examines the intersection of global and national regulatory regimes—analyzing how international human rights and environmental standards have been invoked, adapted, or resisted within the Indian legal-political framework. It explores the roles played by multilateral financial institutions, international NGOs, and transnational solidarity networks in shaping displacement discourse and practice. Further, it evaluates whether these global norms have effectively translated into accountability mechanisms in Jharkhand—or whether they remain symbolic tools in a system marked by deep structural inequality and institutional inertia.

In doing so, the chapter aims to provide a comprehensive understanding of the global-local nexus of displacement, illuminating both the potential and the limitations of international norms in addressing one of India's most pressing developmental paradoxes.

1. International Principles and Guidelines

- United Nations Guiding Principles on Internal Displacement (1998): These principles affirm that development-induced displacement must adhere to international human rights standards. Key principles include informed consent, transparency, non-discrimination, and the right to adequate housing and livelihood.
- ILO Convention 169: While India is not a signatory, this convention emphasizes the rights of Indigenous and Tribal Peoples, especially regarding land, resources, and self-determination.

- UNDRIP (United Nations Declaration on the Rights of Indigenous Peoples, 2007): Recognizes the right of indigenous communities to free, prior, and informed consent (FPIC) before any development or resource exploitation on their lands.

2. Role of International Financial Institutions (IFIs)

- World Bank and ADB Safeguard Policies: These institutions require environmental and social impact assessments, grievance redress mechanisms, and resettlement action plans before funding projects. However, enforcement often remains limited.
- Critiques: Many IFI-funded projects in India, including in Jharkhand, have faced criticism for insufficient rehabilitation and token consultations.

3. India's Legal and Institutional Frameworks

India has constitutional and legislative provisions that can align with international standards:

- Constitutional Rights: Fundamental Rights (Articles 14, 19, 21) and Directive Principles (Articles 38, 39) mandate justice, equality, and protection of marginalized communities.
- PESA and FRA: Although rooted in national law, these acts reflect principles of self-governance, community rights, and informed consent.
- National Human Rights Commission (NHRC): Monitors displacement-related violations and provides recommendations, though its powers are advisory.

4. Gaps and Disconnects

- Weak Enforcement: India's legal frameworks often fall short in implementation. Gram Sabhas are bypassed, and environmental assessments are diluted.
- Judicial Delays: Courts have upheld tribal rights in some cases but often take years to deliver verdicts.
- Lack of Accountability: Government and corporate actors rarely face penalties for violating norms.

5. Towards Convergence: Bridging Global Norms and Local Realities

- Localization of Global Standards: Integrating UN principles into local governance mechanisms such as Gram Sabhas and Panchayats.
- Training and Capacity Building: For bureaucrats, activists, and local leaders to understand and apply international frameworks.
- Participatory Monitoring: Community-based social audits aligned with global best practices.

Conclusion

Global norms and international frameworks—rooted in principles of human rights, environmental justice, and Indigenous sovereignty—offer a valuable scaffolding for envisioning more equitable and accountable models of development. Instruments such as the United Nations Declaration on the Rights of Indigenous Peoples (UNDRIP), the International Labour Organization's Convention 169, and the safeguard policies of institutions like the World Bank and International Finance Corporation (IFC) represent important milestones in the global recognition of the rights of displaced and marginalized communities.

However, the true test of these norms lies not in their articulation but in their implementation. For the displaced communities of Jharkhand, global standards can only be meaningful if they are effectively integrated into national legislation, institutional mechanisms, and—most importantly—local governance practices. The gap between global intent and ground reality often remains vast. Displacement in Jharkhand continues to be marked by limited community consent, inadequate rehabilitation, weak legal enforcement, and tokenistic participation in decision-making processes.

Moreover, structural challenges—such as bureaucratic opacity, corporate collusion, and socio-political marginalization—frequently blunt the impact of global standards. Even when India adopts or endorses international conventions, their domestication into enforceable policy remains uneven. Instruments like the Forest Rights Act (FRA) or PESA, which could operationalize the spirit of global norms, suffer from underutilization, poor implementation, and institutional apathy.

Thus, justice for displaced communities in Jharkhand cannot rest on policy rhetoric alone. It requires robust systems of accountability, transparent grievance redressal mechanisms, strong civil society engagement, and above all, the empowerment of local communities as rights-bearing citizens rather than passive beneficiaries. Genuine participation must replace procedural consultation, and development must shift from being imposed to being collectively imagined and negotiated.

In this light, global norms should be viewed as enabling tools, not substitutes for domestic political will. When strategically leveraged by grassroots movements, civil society actors, and progressive institutions, these norms can reinforce local struggles and amplify the voices of the displaced. But without a corresponding shift in the architecture of power, they risk becoming symbolic gestures in an otherwise exclusionary model of growth.

CHAPTER TEN

Towards an Inclusive Development Paradigm

The preceding chapters have demonstrated that development-induced displacement (DID) in Jharkhand is not an unfortunate by-product or policy failure—it is a systemic and structural outcome of an extractive development paradigm that prioritizes resource exploitation, GDP growth, and infrastructural expansion over the rights, livelihoods, and dignity of marginalized communities. This model, rooted in colonial legacies and perpetuated by post-independence planning, treats land, forests, and minerals as commodities to be harnessed for national progress, often disregarding the cultural, spiritual, and ecological value these hold for Adivasi communities.

Far from being isolated incidents, the displacement of thousands of people across Jharkhand—through dams, mines, industrial corridors, and urbanization—is symptomatic of a deeper contradiction: a model of development that claims to uplift the nation while sacrificing its most vulnerable populations. The voices of displaced Adivasis, their struggles for recognition, their resistance movements, and their alternative visions have laid bare the moral and political crisis at the heart of such development.

In the current global context—marked by escalating climate change, environmental degradation, rising inequality, and growing calls for Indigenous sovereignty and human rights—there is an urgent need to fundamentally rethink the meaning and purpose of development. The dominant growth-centric model has not only proven unsustainable but also deeply unjust, particularly for regions like Jharkhand that are rich in resources yet impoverished in human development indicators.

This moment calls for a paradigm shift—from top-down, extractive development to community-centered, ecologically sustainable, and participatory alternatives. For Jharkhand, this means placing Adivasi worldviews, governance systems, and knowledge at the center of planning and decision-making. It requires moving beyond tokenistic consultations to ensuring free, prior, and informed consent (FPIC); beyond compensation to guaranteeing restitution, rehabilitation, and collective agency; and beyond legal formalism to transforming institutional culture and political will.

A reimagined development framework must prioritize social equity, environmental justice, cultural integrity, and democratic participation. It should value not just economic output, but well-being, resilience, and relationality with nature. It must recognize that displacement is not only a material loss but a disruption of identity, memory, and belonging—and that true development must heal rather than harm.

In this spirit, the path forward for Jharkhand lies in drawing upon its indigenous strengths, listening to its grassroots movements, engaging with global best practices, and building an inclusive model of progress that centers people, not just profit. Only then can development truly become transformative and just—not only for Jharkhand, but as a beacon for other regions grappling with similar tensions.

1. Reimagining Development

Development must move beyond GDP and industrial output as indicators of progress. An inclusive paradigm would prioritize human well-being, ecological sustainability, and cultural integrity. It must center the experiences and aspirations of those most affected—Adivasi communities, women, the poor, and the displaced.

Key principles include:

- People-Centric Planning: Grounded in local knowledge, needs, and participation.
- Sustainable Livelihoods: Emphasizing agroecology, forest-based economies, and decentralized production.
- Ecological Stewardship: Recognizing Adivasis as custodians of biodiversity and forest commons.

2. Policy Recommendations

- Strengthen Legal Protections: Ensure strict enforcement of PESA, FRA, and LARR with teeth against violators.
- Empower Local Institutions: Decentralize planning through empowered Gram Sabhas with binding authority.
- Transparent Benefit Sharing: Communities must have direct stakes in resource royalties and project profits.
- Gender-Just Development: Integrate women's voices in all phases of project design, execution, and evaluation.
- Revamp Resettlement Policies: Go beyond compensation to include land-for-land, cultural restoration, and long-term integration support.

3. Institutional Reforms

- Democratize Decision-Making: Institutionalize Free, Prior, and Informed Consent (FPIC) in law and practice.
- Audit and Accountability: Establish independent bodies to monitor displacement impacts and state-corporate conduct.
- Capacity Building: Train local leaders, bureaucrats, and community members on rights-based frameworks and conflict-sensitive planning.

4. A Vision for Jharkhand

Jharkhand stands at a historic crossroads. The path it chooses will determine not only the fate of its Adivasi communities but the character of development itself in resource-rich yet socially vulnerable regions. The experience of decades of development-induced displacement and extractive growth has made it increasingly clear that the replication of industrial corridors, mega-projects, and mineral-driven economic expansion—without community consent or environmental safeguards—has failed to bring meaningful prosperity to the majority of its people. Instead, it has often exacerbated inequality, eroded cultural heritage, and devastated ecological systems.

A transformative vision for Jharkhand must move beyond the logic of extraction and begin with the understanding that true wealth lies not just beneath the ground but above it—in its forests, rivers, communities, and the knowledge systems that have sustained them for generations. Jharkhand's future does not lie in becoming a carbon copy of industrialized states, but in becoming a model of regionally rooted, ecologically resilient, and socially just development.

A reimagined Jharkhand would:

- Promote regional self-reliance and cooperative enterprises: Instead of depending on multinational corporations or distant capital, Jharkhand can foster community-owned enterprises, producer cooperatives, and decentralized livelihoods in sectors like agro-ecology, forest-based economies, crafts, renewable energy, and sustainable tourism. These models would generate employment, reduce out-migration, and retain wealth within local communities.
- Recognize and nurture diverse forms of knowledge: Adivasi cosmologies, oral traditions, and customary institutions hold valuable insights into sustainable living, conflict resolution, environmental stewardship, and communal welfare. A future-oriented Jharkhand would respect and institutionalize these systems alongside modern scientific and technical knowledge, creating hybrid models of development that are both contextually relevant and globally aware.
- Transition from a policy of displacement to one of dignity, rights, and regeneration: This entails going beyond compensation and resettlement to embrace land restitution, legal empowerment, ecological restoration, and cultural revitalization. A development policy anchored in dignity and justice would ensure that no community is uprooted without consent, and that any change is grounded in meaningful dialogue, participatory planning, and long-term sustainability.

This vision also calls for democratic deepening. Empowering Gram Sabhas, enforcing PESA and Forest Rights Act provisions, and decentralizing resource governance would allow communities to become true custodians of their land and future. The state's role must evolve from that of a broker between capital and land to a guarantor of people's rights, ecological well-being, and intergenerational justice.

Ultimately, Jharkhand has the opportunity to lead the way in redefining development not as conquest, but as care—for people, for the planet, and for future generations. It can become a model not of what India has been, but of what it can become: inclusive, regenerative, and just.

Conclusion: Reclaiming Development, Restoring Justice

Development-induced displacement (DID) is not merely a policy issue or a byproduct of economic progress—it is a profound moral and political test of a society's values. It compels us to ask: *Whose development? At what cost? And who gets to decide?* For too long, the dominant development paradigm in India—and particularly in Jharkhand—has answered these questions in ways that normalize the sacrifice of the few for the perceived prosperity of the many. Entire communities, especially Adivasis, have borne the burden of "nation-building" without ever being invited to define what that nation should look like.

Displacement, then, is not simply the movement of bodies from one place to another—it is the dislocation of histories, the erasure of identities, and the fragmentation of communities. It is an assault on the very principles of justice, democracy, and human dignity that are supposed to underpin modern development. The continued reliance on extractive, centralized, and technocratic models reveals an alarming indifference to the pain and rights of those rendered invisible by grand narratives of progress.

But this reality is not immutable. As this book has shown, resistance persists—in the voices of displaced communities who organize, protest, and dream; in the local movements that reclaim autonomy and ancestral rights; and in the emerging visions of development that are grounded in ecology, equity, and ethics.

Reorienting development requires more than policy reforms or legal safeguards. It demands a transformational shift in our collective imagination—to see development not as the domination of nature and displacement of people, but as the restoration of balance, the recognition of diverse knowledge systems, and the realization of shared well-being. A truly just development process must be participatory, decentralized, and regenerative, one that values people over profits, communities over corporations, and futures over short-term gains.

For Jharkhand, a land rich in both resources and resistance, the challenge is urgent and the opportunity immense. The state can choose to remain a cautionary tale of the resource curse, or it can become a pioneer of alternative development rooted in its indigenous ethos, democratic traditions, and ecological wisdom.

This book, then, is both a critique and a call. A critique of the entrenched systems that perpetuate displacement and injustice, and a call to imagine—and act toward—a future where development empowers rather than uproots, heals rather than harms, and uplifts rather than excludes. It invites policymakers, scholars, activists, and citizens alike to commit to a model of progress that leaves no one behind, and in doing so, truly honors the constitutional and ethical promise of India's democracy.

95

Bibliography, Refernces And Chapterwise Notes

1. Agarwal, Bina. *A Field of One's Own: Gender and Land Rights in South Asia.* Cambridge University Press, 1994.

2. Agrawal, Arun. *Environmentality: Technologies of Government and the Making of Subjects.* Duke University Press, 2005.

3. Ahmad, Imtiaz, ed. *Tribal Development in India: Problems and Prospects.* New Delhi: Mittal Publications, 1991.

4. Baviskar, Amita. *In the Belly of the River: Tribal Conflicts over Development in the Narmada Valley.* Oxford University Press, 2004.

5. Baviskar, Amita. "Written on the Body, Written on the Land: Violence and Environmental Struggles in Central India." *Development and Change* 38, no. 4 (2007): 693-718.

6. Bhaduri, Amit. *Development with Dignity: A Case for Full Employment.* National Book Trust, 2005.

7. Bhaduri, Amit, and Medha Patkar. "Development, Displacement and Rehabilitation: Locating the Victims of Development." *Economic and Political Weekly* 34, no. 47 (1999): 3073-3077.

8. Banerjee-Guha, Swapna, ed. *Accumulation by Dispossession: Transformative Cities in the New Global Order.* Sage, 2010.

9. Banerjee-Guha, Swapna. "Displacement and Development: The Politics of Mining in Jharkhand." *Economic and Political Weekly* 36, no. 30 (2001): 2817-2820.

10. Basu, Kaushik. *An Economist's Miscellany.* Oxford University Press, 2011.

11. Beteille, Andre. *The Backward Classes in Contemporary India.* Oxford University Press, 1992.

12. Beteille, Andre. "The Idea of Indigenous People." *Current Anthropology* 39, no. 2 (1998): 187-192.

13. Bhalla, Sheila. "The Politics of Land Acquisition." *Economic and Political Weekly* 42, no. 22 (2007): 2067-2069.

14. Bhattacharya, Neeladri. "Colonial State and Agrarian Society." In *The Cambridge Economic History of India*, Vol. 2, edited by Dharma Kumar, 28-34. Cambridge University Press, 1983.

15. Bose, Pablo. *Displacement and Citizenship: Histories and Memories of Exclusion.* Oxford University Press, 2020.

16. Cernea, Michael M. *Putting People First: Sociological Variables in Rural*

Development. Oxford University Press, 1985.

17. Cernea, Michael M. "Impoverishment Risks, Risk Management, and Reconstruction: A Model of Population Displacement and Resettlement." *UN Symposium on Hydropower and Sustainable Development*, 2004.

18. Cernea, Michael M., and Christopher McDowell, eds. *Risks and Reconstruction: Experiences of Resettlers and Refugees.* World Bank, 2000.

19. Chakravarti, Anand. *Jharkhand: Underdevelopment and Social Movements.* South Asia Books, 2001.

20. Chopra, Kanchan, and Vikram Dayal. *Displacement, Rehabilitation and Resettlement in India: Land, People and Infrastructure.* Routledge, 2009.

21. Das, Samir Kumar. *Conflict and Peace in India's Northeast: The Role of Civil Society.* East-West Center Washington, 2007.

22. Das, Samir Kumar. *State, Development and Political Culture: Bangladesh and India.* Routledge, 2002.

23. Das, Veena. *Critical Events: An Anthropological Perspective on Contemporary India.* Oxford University Press, 1995.

24. Dandekar, Hemalata, and S. S. Bhagat. "Land Acquisition and Displacement in India: The Reality Check." *Economic and Political Weekly* 47, no. 19 (2012): 163-167.

25. Dreze, Jean, and Amartya Sen. *An Uncertain Glory: India and its Contradictions.* Penguin, 2013.

26. Dreze, Jean, and Amartya Sen. *India: Development and Participation.* Oxford University Press, 2002.

27. Dreze, Jean, and Haris Gazdar. "Uttar Pradesh: The Burden of Inertia." In *Indian Development: Selected Regional Perspectives*, edited by Jean Dreze and Amartya Sen. Oxford University Press, 1997.

28. Escobar, Arturo. *Encountering Development: The Making and Unmaking of the Third World.* Princeton University Press, 1995.

29. Fernandes, Walter. *Development-Induced Displacement in India: National and State Data.* North Eastern Social Research Centre, 2007.

30. Fernandes, Walter. "Development-Induced Displacement: The Class and Gender Perspective." *Social Change* 39, no. 1 (2009): 1-32.

31. Fernandes, Walter, and Enakshi Ganguly Thukral, eds. *Development, Displacement and Rehabilitation: Issues for a National Debate.* Indian Social Institute, 1989.

32. Ferguson, James. *The Anti-Politics Machine: Development, Depoliticization, and Bureaucratic Power in Lesotho.* University of

Minnesota Press, 1994.

33. Gadgil, Madhav, and Ramachandra Guha. *This Fissured Land: An Ecological History of India*. Oxford University Press, 1992.

34. Gadgil, Madhav, and Ramachandra Guha. *Ecology and Equity: The Use and Abuse of Nature in Contemporary India*. Routledge, 1995.

35. Geiser, Urs, and Stephan Rist, eds. *Decentralization Meets Local Complexity: Local Struggles, State Decentralization and Access to Natural Resources in South Asia and Latin America*. Swiss National Centre of Competence in Research, 2009.

36. Guha, Ramachandra. *Savaging the Civilized: Verrier Elwin, His Tribals, and India*. University of Chicago Press, 1999.

37. Guha, Ramachandra. *Environmentalism: A Global History*. Longman, 2000.

38. Guha, Ramachandra, and Madhav Gadgil. "State Forestry and Social Conflict in British India." *Past & Present* 123 (1989): 141-177.

39. Gupta, Akhil. *Postcolonial Developments: Agriculture in the Making of Modern India*. Duke University Press, 1998.

40. Hall, Derek. *Powers of Exclusion: Land Dilemmas in Southeast Asia*. University of Hawaii Press, 2011.

41. Harvey, David. *A Brief History of Neoliberalism*. Oxford University Press, 2005.

42. Harvey, David. *The New Imperialism*. Oxford University Press, 2003.

43. Hirway, Indira, and Amita Shah. "Displacement of Rural Communities in India: Extent, Nature and Policy Issues." *Indian Journal of Agricultural Economics* 56, no. 4 (2001): 1-13.

44. Iyer, Ramaswamy R. *Towards Water Wisdom: Limits, Justice, Harmony*. Sage, 2007.

45. Jha, Praveen. *Land Acquisition and Displacement: Resettlement and Rehabilitation in India—Issues and Challenges*. Springer, 2018.

46. Kothari, Ashish, and Neema Pathak. "Conservation and People: Towards a New Framework." *Economic and Political Weekly* 41, no. 49 (2006): 5242-5252.

47. Kothari, Smitu, and Felix Padel. *Ecology, Economy: Quest for a Socially Informed Connection*. Orient Longman, 1996.

48. Lahiri-Dutt, Kuntala, and Gopa Samanta. *Dams, Displacement and Development: Perspectives from India and China*. Palgrave Macmillan, 2013.

49. Levien, Michael. *Dispossession without Development: Land Grabs in*

Neoliberal India. Oxford University Press, 2018.

50. Levien, Michael. "The Land Question: Special Economic Zones and the Political Economy of Dispossession in India." *Journal of Peasant Studies* 39, no. 3-4 (2012): 933-969.

51. Mahapatra, L.K. *Resettlement, Impoverishment and Reconstruction in India: Development for the Deprived.* Vikas Publishing, 1999.

52. Mahapatra, L.K. "Testing the Risks and Reconstruction Model on India's Resettlement Experiences." In *Risks and Reconstruction,* edited by Michael Cernea and Christopher McDowell, 189-230. World Bank, 2000.

53. Menon, Ajit, and Kanchi Kohli. "Environmental Justice and the Right to Information on Development-Induced Displacement in India." *Development in Practice* 19, no. 6 (2009): 825-836.

54. Mishra, Deepak Kumar. *Displacement, Impoverishment and Exclusion: Political Economy of Development in Jharkhand.* Routledge, 2022.

55. Mohanty, Manoranjan, and Partha Nath Mukherji, eds. *People's Rights: Social Movements and the State in the Third World.* Sage, 1998.

56. Mukherji, Partha Nath. *Structural Transformation and Agrarian Change in India.* Sage, 2014.

57. Nair, Janaki. *Miners and Millhands: Work, Culture and Politics in Princely Mysore.* Sage, 1998.

58. Nilsen, Alf Gunvald. *Dispossession and Resistance in India: The River and the Rage.* Routledge, 2010.

59. Nilsen, Alf Gunvald. "The Politics of Dispossession: Theorizing India's 'Land Wars.'" *Journal of Contemporary Asia* 41, no. 1 (2011): 119-138.

60. Padel, Felix, and Samarendra Das. *Out of This Earth: East India Adivasis and the Aluminium Cartel.* Orient BlackSwan, 2010.

61. Pandey, Gyanendra. *A History of Prejudice: Race, Caste, and Difference in India and the United States.* Cambridge University Press, 2013.

62. Pandey, Gyanendra. *Remembering Partition: Violence, Nationalism and History in India.* Cambridge University Press, 2001.

63. Pathak, Neema. *Community Conserved Areas in India: A Directory.* Kalpavriksh, 2009.

64. Patnaik, Utsa. *The Republic of Hunger and Other Essays.* Merlin Press, 2008.

65. Patnaik, Utsa, and Sam Moyo, eds. *The Agrarian Question in the Neoliberal Era: Primitive Accumulation and the Peasantry.* Pambazuka Press, 2011.

66. Rao, M.S.A., ed. *Social Movements in India: Studies in Peasant, Backward Classes, Sectarian, Tribal and Women's Movements.* Manohar, 1979.

67. Rao, Nitya. "Displacement from Land: Case Studies from Tribal and Non-Tribal Regions in Orissa." *Economic and Political Weekly* 41, no. 50 (2006): 5257-5266.

68. Roy, Arundhati. *The Greater Common Good.* India Book Distributor, 1999.

69. Roy, Arundhati. *Field Notes on Democracy: Listening to Grasshoppers.* Penguin, 2009.

70. Roy, Arundhati. *Capitalism: A Ghost Story.* Haymarket Books, 2014.

71. Roy, Binayak. "Displacement and Rehabilitation in Jharkhand." *Economic and Political Weekly* 38, no. 23 (2003): 2276-2278.

72. Roy, Srirupa. *Beyond Belief: India and the Politics of Postcolonial Nationalism.* Duke University Press, 2007.

73. Roy, Tirthankar. *The Economic History of India 1857–2010.* Oxford University Press, 2011.

74. Sainath, P. *Everybody Loves a Good Drought: Stories from India's Poorest Districts.* Penguin, 1996.

75. Sainath, P. *The Last Heroes: Foot Soldiers of Indian Freedom.* Penguin, 2022.

76. Sahoo, Sarbeswar, and Johannes Quack, eds. *The Public in Public and Private Religions.* Routledge, 2020.

77. Sarin, Madhu. *Disempowered to Empowered: The Struggle for Community Forest Rights in India.* Earthscan, 2014.

78. Sathe, Dhanmanjiri. *Land Acquisition and Compensation in India: Mysteries of Valuation.* Springer, 2017.

79. Scott, James C. *Seeing Like a State: How Certain Schemes to Improve the Human Condition Have Failed.* Yale University Press, 1998.

80. Sen, Amartya. *Development as Freedom.* Oxford University Press, 1999.

81. Sen, Amartya. *Identity and Violence: The Illusion of Destiny.* Penguin, 2006.

82. Shah, Alpa. *In the Shadows of the State: Indigenous Politics, Environmentalism, and Insurgency in Jharkhand, India.* Duke University Press, 2010.

83. Shah, Ghanshyam, ed. *Social Movements and the State.* Sage, 2002.

84. Shah, Ghanshyam, Harsh Mander, S. Bose, and S. Shankar, eds. *Untouchability in Rural India.* Sage, 2006.

85. Sharma, Aradhana. *Logics of Empowerment: Development, Gender, and Governance in Neoliberal India.* University of Minnesota Press, 2008.

86. Sharma, Kiran. "Displacement and Rehabilitation: The Indian

Experience." *Asian Survey* 37, no. 9 (1997): 845-857.

87. Singh, K. S. *The Tribal Situation in India.* Indian Institute of Advanced Study, 1982.

88. Singh, K. S. *Tribal Movements in India.* Manohar, 1983.

89. Singh, Shekhar. "Displacement, Rehabilitation and the Law." *Seminar* 532 (2003): 31-35.

90. Sinha, S. P. *Conflict and Tension in Tribal Society.* Concept Publishing, 1993.

91. Sunder, Nandini. *Subalterns and Sovereigns: An Anthropological History of Bastar (1854–2006).* Oxford University Press, 2007.

92. Sundar, Nandini, ed. *Legal Grounds: Natural Resources, Identity, and the Law in Jharkhand.* Oxford University Press, 2009.

93. Thukral, Enakshi Ganguly, ed. *Big Dams, Displaced People: Rivers of Sorrow, Rivers of Change.* Sage, 1992.

94. Thukral, Enakshi Ganguly, ed. *Displaced by Development: Confronting Marginalisation and Gender Injustice.* Sage, 1996.

95. Upadhyay, Videh. *Handbook on Environmental Law: Forest Laws, Wildlife Laws and the Environment.* LexisNexis Butterworths, 2002.

96. Upadhyay, Videh, and S. Upadhyay. *Forest Laws, Wildlife Laws and the Environment.* LexisNexis, 2002.

97. Verma, R. K. *Jharkhand: Politics of Development and Identity.* Shipra Publications, 2002.

98. Walker, Kenneth. *The Politics of Displacement: Refugees in the Modern World.* Oxford University Press, 1999.

99. World Bank. *Involuntary Resettlement Sourcebook: Planning and Implementation in Development Projects.* World Bank, 2004.

100. Xaxa, Virginius. *State, Society, and Tribes: Issues in Post-Colonial India.* Pearson, 2008.

Notes:

Chapter 01: Theoretical Foundations of Development and Displacement

1. Rostow, W. W. (1960). *The Stages of Economic Growth: A Non-Communist Manifesto.* Cambridge University Press.

2. Sen, Amartya. (1999). *Development as Freedom.* Oxford University Press.

3. Cernea, Michael M. (1997). "Risks, Safeguards and Reconstruction: A Model for Population Displacement and Resettlement." *Economic and Political Weekly*, 32(41), 2879–2888.

4. Harvey, David. (2005). *A Brief History of Neoliberalism.* Oxford University Press.

5. Escobar, Arturo. (1995). *Encountering Development: The Making and Unmaking of the Third World.* Princeton University Press.

6. Xaxa, Virginius. (1999). "Tribes as Indigenous People of India." *Economic and Political Weekly*, 34(51), 3589–3595.

7. D'Costa, Anthony P. (2011). *Development Displacement and Democracy.* Routledge.

8. Sundar, Nandini. (2009). *The Burning Forest: India's War in Bastar.* Juggernaut.

9. Mahapatra, L.K. & Mishra, S. (2018). "Displacement and Rehabilitation in Jharkhand: A Study of Mining and Industrial Projects." *Journal of Development Policy and Practice*, 3(2), 180–198.

10. Padel, Felix & Das, Samarendra. (2010). *Out of This Earth: East India Adivasis and the Aluminium Cartel.* Orient BlackSwan.

11. Banerjee-Guha, Swapna. (2010). *Accumulation by Dispossession.* SAGE Publications.

12. Baviskar, Amita. (2004). *In the Belly of the River.* Oxford University Press.

13. Bhaduri, Amit. (2005). *Development with Dignity.* National Book Trust.

14. Bhattacharya, Neeladri. (1983). "Colonial State and Agrarian Society." *The Cambridge Economic History of India*, Vol. 2.

15. Agarwal, Bina. (1994). *A Field of One's Own: Gender and Land Rights in South Asia.* Cambridge University Press.

16. Agrawal, Arun. (2005). *Environmentality.* Duke University Press.

17. Ahmad, Imtiaz (Ed.). (1991). *Tribal Development in India.* Mittal Publications.

18. Bose, Pablo. (2020). *Displacement and Citizenship.* Oxford University Press.

19. Beteille, Andre. (1992). *The Backward Classes in Contemporary India.* Oxford University Press.

20. Bhalla, Sheila. (2007). "The Politics of Land Acquisition." *EPW*, 42(22), 2067–2069.

21. Fernandes, Walter. (Ed.). (2009). *India's Forced Displacement Policy and Practice.* Indian Social Institute.

22. World Bank. (2004). *Involuntary Resettlement Sourcebook.*

23. UN. (1998). *Guiding Principles on Internal Displacement.*

24. Li, Tania Murray. (2007). *The Will to Improve.* Duke University Press.

25. Scott, James C. (1998). *Seeing Like a State.* Yale University Press.

26. References

27. Cernea, M. M. (1997). The risks and reconstruction model for resettling displaced populations. *World Development, 25*(10), 1569–1587. https://doi.org/10.1016/S0305-750X(97)00054-5

28. D'Costa, A. P. (2011). *A hundred flowers bloom, one hundred schools of thought contend: Ideological undercurrents in China's economic reforms.* Routledge.

29. Escobar, A. (1995). *Encountering development: The making and unmaking of the Third World.* Princeton University Press.

30. Harvey, D. (2005). *A brief history of neoliberalism.* Oxford University Press.

31. Mahapatra, L. K., & Mishra, S. (2018). *Displacement, rehabilitation and resettlement in India: Policies, practices and experiences.* Routledge India.

32. Padel, F., & Das, S. (2010). *Out of this earth: East India Adivasis and the aluminium cartel.* Orient BlackSwan.

33. Rostow, W. W. (1960). *The stages of economic growth: A non-communist manifesto.* Cambridge University Press.

34. Sen, A. (1999). *Development as freedom.* Oxford University Press.

35. Sundar, N. (2009). *The Sundar Committee Report on Koel-Karo: The politics of development and displacement.* In Fernandes, W. (Ed.), *India's forced displacement policy and practice: Is compensation up to its functions?* (pp. 155–178). Indian Social Institute.

36. Xaxa, V. (1999). Tribes as Indigenous People of India. *Economic and Political Weekly, 34*(51), 3589–3595.

37. Cernea, M. M. (1997). *Risks, Safeguards and Reconstruction: A Model for Population Displacement and Resettlement.* Economic and Political Weekly, 32(41), 2879-2888.

38. Sen, A. (1999). *Development as Freedom.* Oxford University Press.

39. Baviskar, A. (1995). In the Belly of the River: Tribal Conflicts over Development in the Narmada Valley. Oxford University Press.

40. Escobar, A. (1995). *Encountering Development: The Making and Unmaking of the Third World.* Princeton University Press.

41. Xaxa, V. (1999). Tribes as Indigenous People of India. Economic and Political Weekly, 34(51), 3589-3595.

42. Sundar, N. (2009). *The Burning Forest: India's War in Bastar.* Juggernaut.

43. Mahapatra, L. K., & Mishra, S. (2018). Displacement and Rehabilitation in Jharkhand: A Study of Mining and Industrial Projects. *Journal of Development Policy and Practice, 3*(2), 180-198.

44. Padel, F., & Das, S. (2010). Out of This Earth: East India Adivasis and the Aluminium Cartel. Orient Blackswan.

45. Harvey, D. (2005). *A Brief History of Neoliberalism.* Oxford University Press.

46. D'Costa, A. (2011). Development Displacement and Democracy: The Politics of Land and Refugees in India. *Journal of Asian Studies*, 70(4), 1117-1144.

Chapter 02: Understanding Development-Induced Displacement

1. Cernea, M. M. (1997). "The Risks and Reconstruction Model." *World Development*, 25(10), 1569–1587.

2. Escobar, A. (1995). *Encountering Development.* Princeton University Press.

3. Sen, A. (1999). *Development as Freedom.* Oxford University Press.

4. Rostow, W. W. (1960). *The Stages of Economic Growth.* Cambridge University Press.

5. Harvey, D. (2005). *A Brief History of Neoliberalism.* Oxford University Press.

6. Padel & Das. (2010). *Out of This Earth.* Orient Black Swan.

7. Xaxa, V. (1999). "Tribes as Indigenous People." *EPW*, 34(51), 3589–3595.

8. Sundar, N. (2009). "Koel-Karo and Politics of Displacement." In *India's Forced Displacement Policy and Practice*, ed. W. Fernandes.

9. Mahapatra, L. K. (2018). *Displacement and Rehabilitation in Jharkhand.*

10. D'Costa, A. (2011). *Development Displacement and Democracy.* Routledge.

11. Padel, F. (2010). *Sacrificing People: Invasions of a Tribal Landscape.* Orient Longman.

12. Baviskar, A. (1995). *In the Belly of the River.* Oxford University Press.

13. Agarwal, Bina. (1994). *A Field of One's Own.* Cambridge University Press.

14. Scott, J. C. (1998). *Seeing Like a State.* Yale University Press.

15. Bhaduri & Patkar. (1999). "Development and Rehabilitation." *EPW*, 34(47).

16. Shah, Ghanshyam. (2004). *Social Movements in India.* SAGE Publications.

17. Saxena, N. C. (2005). *Forests and Tribals.* Planning Commission Report.

18. National R&R Policy, 2007. Government of India.

19. Roy, Arundhati. (1999). "The Greater Common Good." *Outlook Magazine.*
20. Bhattacharjee, J. (2000). "Legal Framework for Displacement." *Economic and Political Weekly.*
21. Baviskar, A. (2007). "Written on the Body." *Development and Change,* 38(4).
22. Fernandes, Walter. (2007). *Development-Induced Displacement in India: Problems and Policies.*
23. Basu, Kaushik. (2011). *An Economist's Miscellany.* Oxford University Press.
24. UNDRIP (2007).
25. World Bank. (2017). *Environmental and Social Framework.*

Chapter 03: Adivasi Communities and Structural Exclusion

1. Xaxa, V. (1999). *EPW,* 34(51), 3589–3595.
2. Baviskar, A. (2004). *In the Belly of the River.* Oxford University Press.
3. Padel & Das. (2010). *Out of This Earth.*
4. Sundar, N. (2009). *The Burning Forest.* Juggernaut.
5. Shah, A. (2010). *In the Shadows of the State.* Duke University Press.
6. Mahapatra, L. K. (2018). "Rehabilitation in Jharkhand."
7. Rao, M. S. A. (1978). *Social Movements in India.*
8. Corbridge, S. (1995). *Development Studies.* Polity Press.
9. Forest Rights Act, 2006.
10. PESA Act, 1996.
11. The Fifth Schedule of the Indian Constitution.
12. Roy, Arundhati. (2010). "Walking with the Comrades."
13. Bhagat, R. B. (2013). "Resettlement and Urban Marginality."
14. Ali, S. (2005). *Tribal Movements in Jharkhand.*
15. Beteille, Andre. (1998). "Idea of Indigenous People."
16. Guha, Ramachandra. (1989). *The Unquiet Woods.*
17. Misra, Udayon. (2000). *India's Northeast.*
18. Chowdhury, S. (2013). "Tribal Displacement in the Coal Belt."
19. Tiwari, M. (2009). "Tribal Livelihood and State Policies."
20. Bhaduri, A. (2005). *Development with Dignity.*
21. Sinha, S. (2010). "State Formation and Resistance in Jharkhand."
22. Chakravarti, A. (2001). "Land Acquisition in India."
23. Ali, A. (2015). *Tribal Identity and Resource Politics.*

24. Ota, A. B. (2000). "Tribal Development and Displacement."
25. Rao, V. (2006). "Cultural Politics of Displacement."

Chapter 04: Jharkhand's Political Economy and the Resource Curse

1. Sachs, Jeffrey & Warner, Andrew. (1995). "Natural Resource Abundance and Economic Growth."
2. Ross, Michael. (2001). "Does Oil Hinder Democracy?" *World Politics.*
3. Mahapatra & Mishra. (2018). *Journal of Development Policy and Practice.*
4. Sundar, N. (2009). *The Burning Forest.*
5. D'Costa, A. (2011). *Development Displacement and Democracy.*
6. Baviskar, A. (2004). *In the Belly of the River.*
7. Xaxa, V. (1999). *EPW,* 34(51).
8. Padel & Das. (2010). *Out of This Earth.*
9. Harvey, D. (2005). *A Brief History of Neoliberalism.*
10. Cernea, M. M. (1997). *World Development,* 25(10).
11. Roy, Arundhati. (1999). "The Greater Common Good."
12. Guha, R. (1989). *The Unquiet Woods.*
13. Agarwal, Bina. (1994). *A Field of One's Own.*
14. Fifth Schedule of the Constitution.
15. PESA, 1996.
16. Forest Rights Act, 2006.
17. District Mineral Foundation Rules.
18. MMDR Act.
19. World Bank Environmental and Social Framework.
20. Saxena, N. C. (2010). "Tribal Land Rights."
21. Das, P. (2012). "Coal Mining and Tribal Life."
22. Shah, Ghanshyam. (2004). *Social Movements in India.*
23. Tilly, C. (2003). *The Politics of Collective Violence.*
24. Oommen, T. K. (2010). *Reconciliation in Post-Conflict Societies.*
25. Bhaduri, A. (2005). *Development with Dignity.*

Chapter 05: Understanding Development-Induced Displacement (Field-Level and Legal Analysis)

1. Cernea, M. M. (2004). *UN Symposium on Hydropower.*
2. National Rehabilitation & Resettlement Policy (2007).
3. FRA (2006).

4. PESA (1996).

5. Land Acquisition Act (1894) and LARR Act (2013).

6. Xaxa, V. (1999). *EPW*, 34(51).

7. Baviskar, A. (2007). *Development and Change*, 38(4).

8. Fernandes, Walter. (2007). *India's Forced Displacement Policy and Practice.*

9. UN Guiding Principles on Internal Displacement (1998).

10. UNDRIP (2007).

11. World Bank Involuntary Resettlement Policy.

12. Mahapatra, L. K. (2018). *Jharkhand Displacement Studies.*

13. Padel & Das. (2010). *Out of This Earth.*

14. TISS Reports on Koel-Karo Dam.

15. Roy, Arundhati. (1999). "The Greater Common Good."

16. Dandekar, H. C. (2011). "Resettlement Strategies in India."

17. Ramanathan, Usha. (2008). "Land Acquisition and Law."

18. Sainath, P. (2009). *Everybody Loves a Good Drought.*

19. Shah, A. (2010). *In the Shadows of the State.*

20. Forest Survey of India Reports.

21. Census of India (2011).

22. UNDP Reports on Indigenous Peoples.

23. Scott, James C. (1998). *Seeing Like a State.*

24. Sinha, A. (2009). "Gender and Displacement."

25. CSE Reports on Jharkhand Mining.

Chapter 06: Field Realities: Voices from Displaced Communities

1. Baviskar, Amita. *In the Belly of the River.* Oxford University Press, 2004.

2. Fernandes, Walter. *India's Forced Displacement Policy and Practice.* Indian Social Institute, 2007.

3. Cernea, Michael M. "Risks, Safeguards and Reconstruction." *EPW*, 32(41), 1997.

4. Shah, Alpa. *In the Shadows of the State.* Duke University Press, 2010.

5. Mahapatra, L.K., & Mishra, S. (2018). *Displacement and Rehabilitation in Jharkhand.*

6. Padel, Felix & Das, Samarendra. *Out of This Earth.* Orient BlackSwan, 2010.

7. Sundar, Nandini. *The Burning Forest.* Juggernaut, 2009.

8. Roy, Arundhati. "The Greater Common Good." *Outlook*, 1999.

9. Xaxa, Virginius. (1999). "Tribes as Indigenous People of India." *EPW*, 34(51).

10. FRA (2006).

11. PESA (1996).

12. LARR Act (2013).

13. World Bank. *Involuntary Resettlement Sourcebook*, 2004.

14. Pathak, Neema & Kothari, Ashish. "Community Rights and Governance." *EPW*, 2006.

15. TISS Reports on Subarnarekha Dam Displacement.

16. NTPC Land Acquisition Report, Jharkhand.

17. Indian Social Institute. *Case Studies in Displacement*.

18. Sainath, P. *Everybody Loves a Good Drought*. Penguin India, 1996.

19. JIPF Reports on Cultural Displacement.

20. BIRSA Documentation Archives.

21. UNDP. *Human Development Report on Jharkhand Tribals*, 2015.

22. Singh, K.S. (1993). *Tribal Society in India*.

23. Bijoy, C.R. "Forest Rights Struggles." *EPW*, 2003.

24. Das, Bikas C. "Women and Displacement in Jharkhand."

25. Sharma, S. "Identity Ruptures and Relocation."

Chapter 07: Resistance, Resilience, and Policy Responses

1. Baviskar, Amita. (2007). "Written on the Body, Written on the Land." *Development and Change*, 38(4).

2. Sundar, Nandini. *The Burning Forest*. Juggernaut, 2009.

3. Koel-Karo Jan Sangathan Reports.

4. Pathalgadi Movement Pamphlets & Legal Submissions.

5. Netarhat Anti-Firing Range Archive.

6. Fifth Schedule of the Constitution of India.

7. Forest Rights Act (2006).

8. Panchayats (Extension to Scheduled Areas) Act (1996).

9. LARR Act (2013).

10. National Human Rights Commission Reports on Displacement.

11. Shah, Ghanshyam. *Social Movements in India*. SAGE, 2004.

12. Tilly, Charles. *The Politics of Collective Violence*. Cambridge University Press, 2003.

13. Rao, M.S.A. *Social Movements in India*.

14. Bindrai Institute Reports.

15. JIPF (Jharkhand Indigenous Peoples' Forum).
16. Roy, Arundhati. "Walking with the Comrades." *Outlook*, 2010.
17. Hirway, Indira & Shah, Amita. "Displacement of Rural Communities."
18. Levien, Michael. *Dispossession without Development*. Oxford University Press, 2018.
19. Kumar, Kundan. "Politics of Resistance in Jharkhand."
20. Ekta Parishad Documentation.
21. Gupta, Akhil. *Postcolonial Developments*.
22. Singh, Binayak. "Grassroots Democracy and Resistance."
23. UAPA Case Law Archive (related to activists).
24. Social Watch India. *State of Governance Report*.
25. Bhaduri, Amit. *Development with Dignity*.

Chapter 08: Global Norms and India's Institutional Framework

1. United Nations Guiding Principles on Internal Displacement (1998).
2. UNDRIP (2007).
3. ILO Convention 169.
4. World Bank. *Environmental and Social Framework* (2017).
5. IFC. *Performance Standards on Environmental and Social Sustainability*.
6. ADB Safeguard Policy Statement (2009).
7. FRA (2006).
8. PESA (1996).
9. National Human Rights Commission (NHRC) Reports.
10. LARR Act (2013).
11. Forest Survey of India Reports.
12. CERD (UN Committee on Elimination of Racial Discrimination) Observations.
13. UNDP. *Indigenous Peoples and Governance*.
14. Mahapatra, L.K. "Resettlement and International Norms."
15. Amnesty International Reports on India's Displacement Cases.
16. Human Rights Watch (2005). *Out of Sight: Displacement and Injustice*.
17. Padel & Das. *Out of This Earth*.
18. Escobar, Arturo. *Encountering Development*.
19. Cernea, Michael. "Impoverishment, Risk and Reconstruction."
20. Kothari, Smitu. "Development and Human Rights." *EPW*, 1996.
21. UN Habitat Reports on Displacement.
22. CSE India. *Green Tribunal and Indigenous Rights*.

23. Report of the UN Special Rapporteur on the Rights of Indigenous Peoples.

24. International Rivers. *Dam-Induced Displacement Global Survey.*

25. Social Impact Assessment Toolkit – UNDP India.

Chapter 09: Towards an Inclusive Development Paradigm

1. Sen, Amartya. *Development as Freedom.* Oxford University Press, 1999.

2. D'Costa, Anthony P. *Development Displacement and Democracy.* Routledge, 2011.

3. Cernea, Michael M. *Putting People First.* Oxford University Press, 1985.

4. Padel & Das. *Out of This Earth.*

5. Escobar, A. *Encountering Development.*

6. Bhaduri, A. *Development with Dignity.*

7. Baviskar, A. *In the Belly of the River.*

8. Guha, Ramachandra & Gadgil, Madhav. *Ecology and Equity.* Routledge, 1995.

9. Agrawal, Arun. *Environmentality.* Duke University Press, 2005.

10. Ferguson, James. *The Anti-Politics Machine.*

11. Levien, Michael. *Dispossession without Development.*

12. Kothari, Ashish & Pathak, Neema. "Alternatives to Development." *EPW.*

13. Gandhi, P.V. "Eco-Socialism in India."

14. Banerjee-Guha, S. *Accumulation by Dispossession.*

15. Xaxa, V. "Tribes as Indigenous People." *EPW.*

16. Lal, Anupam. "Inclusive Development Metrics."

17. Roy, Arundhati. "Reclaiming the Commons."

18. UNDP. *Sustainable Human Development Report.*

19. World Social Forum Declarations.

20. Indigenous Terra Madre Reports (Slow Food Movement).

21. FAO. *Indigenous Peoples and Sustainable Development.*

22. UNEP. *Greening the Economy with Indigenous Knowledge.*

23. Chakravarti, A. "Democracy and Displacement."

24. Global Tapestry of Alternatives Initiative.

25. Lal, Vinay. "Beyond Development." *Seminar* Journal.